Strange Journey

The vision life of a psychic Indian woman.

Louise Lone Dog is of Mohawk and Delaware Indian ancestry, and lives in New York State. She is one of the first Native Americans to write with vivid detail about the spiritual and psychic knowledge and power possessed by many of her people. She is a mystic, a seer and a prophet, and through her vision she brings back the original wisdom of the ancients. In this revised edition, she reveals truth and prophecy received through Spirit for this pivotal moment in history. She does so because of the desperate urgency to rouse all people to find their own spiritual strength and knowledge in this time, when mankind hovers so agonizingly on the brink of a new age of peace built on spiritual rebirth and the unity of all creation. We hope that you will find, as we do, that her deep sincerity, wisdom, and goodness is contagious and inspiring.

Strange Journey

Journey

The vision life of a psychic Indian woman.

by Louise Lone Dog

edited by Patricia Powell
illustrated by Tso Yazzy (Chester Kahn), Navajo

Naturegraph Publishers, Inc.
Happy Camp, California

Books for a better world

Library of Congress Cataloguing in Publication Data

Lone Dog, Louise.
    Strange journey : the vision life of a psychic Indian woman / by
Louise Lone Dog ; edited by Patricia Powell ; illustrated by Tso
Yazzy (Chester Kahn).
        p.   cm.
    ISBN 0-87961-206-1 : $15.95. -- ISBN 0-87961-207-X (pbk.) : $8.95
    1. Lone Dog, Louise. 2. Psychics--United States--Biography.
3. Mohawk Indians--Biography. 4. Delaware Indians--Biography.
5. Indians of North America--Religion and mythology.   I. Powell,
Patricia.   II. Title.
BF1027.L63A3   1989
133.8'092--dc20
[B]   89-13484
                                                                CIP

BF
1027
.L63
A3
1989

Naturegraph Publishers, Inc.
3543 Indian Creek Road
Happy Camp, California 96039
U.S.A.

Books for a better world

*This book is dedicated to
the Warriors of the Rainbow—
all those who seek to revive the human spirit
by love and understanding.*

Table of Contents

Foreword

Many years ago my grandfather, Charles Bender, helped found the first independent bank in the state of Nevada, the Washoe County Bank of Reno. Those were the years of the rough and rugged west (1860's to early 1900's), and my grandfather ran his bank on the basis of his judgment of character in the men who came to do business with him, loaning money to those he trusted and refusing it to those he did not. He rarely made a mistake in this judgment, for he had keen eyes and he looked for the telltale signs in a man's face that tell of hidden weaknesses.

When Louise Lone Dog sent us the manuscript of her book, **Strange Journey,** I was afraid that we might be getting something dreamed up, with no basis in fact. Since it was about a subject whose nature was very hard to prove one way or the other, I felt a bit like a man getting out for the first time on a tightrope, high above the ground. However, in getting acquainted with this wonderful new Indian friend, we became aware of a vital personality, through which shone the very essence of truthfulness and love and wisdom. I could not look at the picture of her face without feeling very strongly, as my grandfather must have felt when he looked on the faces of certain men, that here was the very embodiment of honesty. I knew also that I saw in that face the humble and yet powerful desire to obey the will of our Great Maker.

Science is only beginning to understand a little of the nature of the sixth sense called extrasensory perception, and many scientists are reluctant to admit even that little. But the whole history of science has shown again and again how often the incredible and impossible have been proved true. I believe, from considerable experience, that many Indians are very psychic, but they are very shy about showing this power because of the laughter and ridicule from ignorant people. Here, at last, is one Indian who speaks frankly of this strange power, and her words flow with the Spirit.

Vinson Brown, Naturegraph

Chapter 1

Wilderness Ways

"I am as free as Nature first made man,
Ere the base laws of servitude began,
When wild in woods the noble savage ran."
John Dryden

My ancestry is of the Mohawk and Delaware peoples. The Delaware or Lenni-Lenape, as they were also called, were famous for their mystic qualities and psychic abilities. My papa and mama I most admire for the way they held on to the best qualities of their ancestors, practiced what was beautiful in the ancient ways, and taught me and my brothers and sisters to seek for the Great Spirit in a study of nature and a meditation in the silence.

From time immemorial the primitive races, as they are sometimes called, lived very close to nature and recognized the Great Spirit or God power in every living thing in the whole universe. So my Indian ancestors roamed the hills, the valleys and the plains for many centuries, observing and studying carefully the life of the many animals on both land and sea. They naturally observed the plants closely and gained much knowledge of the use of all kinds of vegetation. With such intimate knowledge, it became easy to recognize that wise and spiritual teachings were brought through Mother Nature to both men and animals. Watching Mother Nature, they learned the uses of various flowers, buds, herbs, roots, barks, oils and soils for foods and for cures for various ills.

The medicine man or woman was gifted with a greater than average knowledge of the many cures from the different plants, and had an inborn sense, known as the "natural touch," by which they could sense ways to heal and help people. That gift, like many family traits, often is handed down through generations. My papa was a medicine man, and my mama had many wonderful psychic powers.

The many, many rare and well-kept remedies at times are passed down to others in the family, but more than often the gift is allowed to develop naturally by the one that is in tune with this type of work from a very early age, since healing is a gift of our Great Spirit Creator and rarely to be taught in true fullness to other men. If a medicine man or woman lost too many patients or was unable to cure them, their practice was soon lost, since few could or would believe them, knowing they were not spiritually gifted.

In primitive days nature's garden and its fertility were not injured by harmful chemicals, nor was the food hurt by its artificial flavoring, dehydrating and other processes by which machines and the men who operate them prepare food for display and sale in our supermarkets. With nature's garden growing in abundance and the fertile soil bringing forth pure crops, the Indians found plenty of nourishment. In primitive days one found the time to pound the many nuts, grains, beans, bark and roots and use them for meal in cooking bread, puddings, and other dainties.

Juices were pounded or pressed out of many vegetables and fruits. Berries, roots, bark and leaves were mixed with meats in such a combination as pemmican. Of course, when the foods were in season, and, while roaming the hills, valleys and plains, it was easier to pick the many ripe fruits or vegetables, ready to eat, right off the plant, tree, bush or vine. There was less cooking of foods than today, though modern research is showing us that many vegetables and fruits are more healthy when eaten raw.

A life in the open gave more time for watching nature in its budding and blooming seasons and to observe the many animals and insects at work or play. Harvest time during the Indian summer was a most joyful period. While spending much time under the blue skies, the Indian learned to copy many of the good habits of the animals, birds, and insects while watching them, as Mother Nature changed her seasons.

The wise ones among the Indians taught the children and others not only what foods were good for them and how to prepare them, but how to dance and play in the sunlight for health, how to avoid excessive sunburn that can shorten life, and how never to overtax one's strength by becoming too daring or by otherwise disobeying the laws of nature. Thus, those working out in the sun all day long, wore a covering over the head and the tender parts of the body to avoid over-exposure to the strong sunlight of summer, and so also when they went swimming.

Knowing that a higher power directed the courses of the heavenly bodies, the movements of the seas, rivers, and lakes, as well as other parts of his creation, the Indians worshipped the supreme light of the world, which is the Great Spirit Mystery, with prayer, songs and dances, expressing humbleness, love and joy. Neither the sun nor the moon or any of the planets were ever worshipped, as the Indian knew these were merely symbols of the greater power. Expressing a happy, worshipful heart, many dances were from nature. Such dances as the sun dance, the green corn dance, the bear dance, the buffalo trot, the eagle dance, the squirrel dance, the snake dance, all expressed a nature theme.

> "Praise the Lord!
> Praise him with timbrel and dance;
> Praise him with strings and pipe!"
> from the 150th Psalm; Revised Standard Version

Our Great Creator placed everything on the land, in the sea, in the earth, and in the many bodies of water for all of his creatures, giving them nourishment and medicinal properties in their natural form. There are a few little germs in everybody, but by eating right and thinking right and acting right you prevent those germs from developing in a healthy body and mind.

In a weak body that is undernourished, any disease can run rampant and will eventually destroy both body and mind. Mankind is created from the soil or humus (hence the name human), and turns to the earth and bodies of water to find the many things that keep the body and mind healthy for many years of activity.

"With long life will I satisfy him and show him my salvation."

from the 91st Psalm

The spiritual life known by many of the primitives helped them prepare for changing to a higher plane by striving through right food, right exercise and right thoughts to live a sound, happy, healthy life. To such people age means little.

You should uproot the weed of thinking you are old, since in spirit you are always young. When anyone calls you old, you just answer, "How old is old?" You just think of a beautiful, sturdy oak tree that stands many years shedding its leaves and blooming again. This old-age-decrepit talk is like a contagious disease floating around everywhere, but we can easily rise above such nonsense talk, as the ancients of the Indians did, by saying the spirit mind is ever young, as long as it allows the Great Spirit to shine through. Not only does the spirit heal, but it also teaches us what to do and eat, just at the right time.

The Indians of the old days knew the earth and all its creatures by learning to watch for the slightest movement and interpret it correctly, by listening for every sound and vibration with a keen ear and a keen mind, and by knowing the meaning of every smell and taste and touch. From this highly developed keenness of the senses, many of them moved on to a knowledge of the sixth sense, the sense of the spirit world, and saw and understood things beyond space and time and place in a way the modern, civilized man, with his dulled senses and his emphasis on material luxury and pleasure, finds hard to grasp or understand. It is truly due to ignorance for such people to say the sixth sense does not exist when they have neither made any attempt to understand it nor to practice those disciplines of the mind and body that might make them aware of its existence.

The very names of the Indians, such as Running Bear, Ghost Dog, Many Moons, Red Cloud, Spotted Calf, Rainbow, Morning Star, and Wolf Medicine, attest to their vision life and spirit.

When the Indians of earlier times went into the silence in the wilderness to seek for this spirit, they purified every thought and action through rigorous physical exercise and powerful mental training, plus fasting and praying. To such people the spirit came so strongly that they went down from the mountains and hills literally reborn. Chastity and purity, love and kindness, courage and vigor, honesty and trustworthiness, became as much a part of their lives as their arms or legs. So it must be in this time too, if men and women are once again to be worthy of their Creator, and for the world to enter a new golden age.

Chapter 2

An Indian Child and the Spirit World

"The sublimest song to be heard on earth is the lisping of the human soul on the lips of children."

Victor Hugo

From early childhood and right at my mama's knee I began to ask many questions. A favorite question was, "How did the early primitives learn to study without books?" Mama had studied to be a school teacher and Papa had traveled quite a great deal, and I was sure that they could answer many questions that seemed to come from within.

Hearing Mama tell us to "get out under the blue sky and listen often to nature's teachings," I began to understand how the early Indians studied nature and learned what to eat and what not to eat and even how to act by watching the animals. Papa taught us about plants by allowing us to watch him plant his garden and then encouraging each of us to plant a little garden too.

To get out under the blue sky and listen to nature's teachings was the first instruction. A constant change of scenery was another lesson to remember. When taking a walk or stroll, we were taught to look for everything the new view would bring in the way of interesting thoughts and understandings to the mind. Still another lesson taught very early was never to kill anything until we were sure it was a pest of some kind, or dangerous. Most creatures we left alone, as Great Spirit's creations, and, when we killed for food, we did so with a prayer for forgiveness and asking the Great Mystery to help these creatures in the spirit world.

Very early we began to notice that many animals sensed danger or the attitudes of people around them by other means than the usual five senses. Many, including dogs, cats and horses, had this sixth sense highly developed.

We had cats, dogs and chickens, and Mama had names for most of them, though Papa added names to some of our pets. Our first cat, Hanna, came before I was born. Then we had Cura Patkin, Rumpelstiltskin, Gilpin Horner, and Philanese. Another set of kittens Mama named Jeremiah, Spitzbergen, Jervace Manhattan, Susie Annie, Annie Belle, and Cinderella Rinemie. Then there was Mr. Hemstager and others named Don Arty, Tippie Toe, Tommy Cat, and Tougaloo. My own Indian childhood name, meaning "my pet," was Pusadil!

We had dogs, including Tops, a part birddog and part shepherd, also Siney, Bepo, and Fluffy. Fluffy used to ruffle up the covers on the bed if he wasn't taken out, since he didn't care to stay home and watch the house. But Fluffy was a good watch dog and knew how to get his way. Tops enjoyed outings, but he did not mind watching the house and keeping the cats in line when we were gone for the day or evening.

Tommy Cat and Tabby were the ones he mostly took charge of, and they obeyed him very well. Sometimes Tops would be lying near them with his paws spread forward, greeting us with a bark but guarding them until we said, "Tops, you have done a very good job of watching the home, and now you can let us take over."

Even when we were home, at times, the different cats would have a race around the house, and, if Tops was sleeping, they would go after his tail and paw at it just to wake him up. When he got too annoyed, he would back them up into a corner and lie right in front of them, half nodding but watching them. If they made a crooked move or tried to slink away, he would give out one bark and they would settle back, knowing that he meant business and, in no time at all, they too would fall asleep and all would be peaceful.

Before we moved to New York City, we had a large yard with apple trees, peach trees, and a large space where Papa raised his garden and I had a space to raise mine. Around that time there was a man who delivered buttermilk to us, and we always had a big jug ready for the time he arrived. I haven't tasted buttermilk like that since we moved from that city. And rarely do we get the fine garden vegetables with the wonderful taste, such as we had from that garden. It is only when friends bring in different vegetables from the country, home raised, that we have the tasty salads now. In those days, on nice evenings, we all gathered together and took long walks. We often rushed off to see celebrations and parades, particularly liking to follow the Scotch bands.

I can still see in my mind Papa's garden and what a wonderful gardener he was, so often bringing in a great array of fresh vegetables from our garden, and it has made me think many times how much healthier and happier every family would be if they would just have such a garden for food, observation, and exercise.

But we had just as much enjoyment watching nature growing in the spring and summer and observing all of the Creator's creatures, big or small. I would spend hours tending my little garden, then spend time watching the little insects at work, such as the ants or bees. Often, we searched for plant foods. Breaking a little sunflower apart, we ate the seeds after shelling them, and found many other plants to eat, though, first Mama or Papa were always asked to make sure it was good.

As children, we learned that some plants were poisonous, but the wise people knew how to take the poison out of certain ones to make them good to eat. We left such plants alone until we were shown how to use them. While picking berries of many kinds, we were warned of snakes, but our parents knew how to handle snakes, and told us to stay in the background at such times. They also taught us to watch the animals, and, if a cat or dog wasn't feeling well, to let it outside where it could find the plants or minerals it needed to cure itself. We would often bring the plant to our parents, wanting to know if it was good for us to eat too. Thus we were trained in the way of the Indians to seek many of the things the animals used for food and medical healing.

In those early days we always drank very tasty herbal teas and I remember my mama and papa telling me how Great Aunt Serena, who lived to be far beyond a hundred years, taught them how to use many wonderful herbs in teas. It was at a much later time, that we began to forget about using these teas because of living in a great city. When I began to get a pimply face and the regular medicines of the doctor didn't help, the spirits of Papa and Great Aunt Serena began to tell me to go back to these teas and more fresh vegetables and fruits. When I did, the pimples soon began to disappear. We loved Aunt Serena's herbal teas, and their mixtures. How we loved to blend many of them for dinner or for a nice tea-time drink. It was wonderful to start making these fine teas again and also to taste once more the marvelous graham biscuits we had eaten in childhood.

Mama said Aunt Serena always spoke of the Great Spirit, and lived life as he wants one to live, and, even at the great age of much more than a hundred when Mama knew her, she stood just as straight as an arrow.

The primitive Indians always put fish, and fruit and vegetable rinds, along with manure and leaf mold, around plants they were raising for food, thus keeping the soil fertile and the plants healthy, so that the attacks of insects and disease were not apt to harm them. Our people never used such things as sprays and chemicals, which may be harmful to man, but depended on the natural fertilizers to build strong and healthy plants that would pour the pure essence of health into our bloodstreams.

We and our ancestors truly learned from nature as children, and it is very sad to see so few parents these days taking their children out into the open at all times of the year to teach them the things of nature or even letting them learn themselves. How few indeed even take the time to point out some beautiful sunrise or sunset and give the soul time to absorb from this beauty some of the spirit of the universe. No wonder jangled nerves of worldly people, who have never learned the peace and understanding of nature, often resent the tune of nature's serenade when they come to the country and even become annoyed at the sound of a chirping bird or a cricket!

But very early in childhood I began to hear the inner spirit voice and, with a prayer in my heart, I was awakened to light and to an understanding of nature. From my earliest years, I would often find myself looking into the mirror of the spirit world, seeing many spirit friends and speaking to them as naturally as I would to any friend in life. At that early stage in my life I thought that everyone had this gift. How happy I was when, as I realized I lived between the world of the spirit and this world, I saw in that other world some of the reflection of the Great Spirit.

When feeling the presence of a spirit or seeing anything "supernatural" when a child, I never failed to tell my family, from the very beginning, of these experiences. I've often wondered since about other children who have had and are having somewhat similar experiences, and wonder what their parents say to them, since there must be many with such experiences.

What some people call imaginary playmates in childhood are indeed very real spirit playmates. I had such a playmate for several years. I was happy when my playmate came to visit and this special one came often; then one day he went away and never came back again. It was many a day after that that I would wait for him to come and play and, for some time, I could not help but wonder what had happened to him, where he had moved and why he hadn't warned me when his family was moving away. Not being allowed to wander far from home and having a large yard to play in, where all the neighborhood children came to play, we never thought of their exact addresses or questioned where some lived, knowing that they could not live too far from the immediate neighborhood.

One day, while speaking to my sister about his long absence, to my surprise she spoke up, telling me, "No one has ever seen your playmate you call 'Johnny.' You can ask any of them, and none of the family has ever seen him except you. We have all been curious, wondering how long these visits with Johnny would last, and we have all been wondering who he was. Now we can tell you that he was a spirit, since he is gone and hasn't been back for a while."

This statement really startled me. Being a child that had had a few other experiences not quite understood at the time, I was more puzzled than ever. This experience with a spirit playmate that the others hadn't seen had been so vivid and real to me, as if he were exactly like any other living pal of mine.

I had played with my spirit friend for months which went into years, in and out of the house, and to think that no one else but me had seen him completely astounded me. Mama then showed me that my experiences with the spirit world were known to her when I was only a tiny child. She recalled a time when I was just beginning to walk and talk when a door had opened and something or someone had come into the room with whom I immediately had a pleasant conversation. She said that when I finished the friendly talk, I ran out to play, forgetting all about the incident, which had, however, amazed her so much she never forgot it. Years later, Mama told me that the former owners of our house had had a little boy who passed away before we occupied it. It seems the neighbors had mentioned this little boy to her. I soon understood that my childhood playmate must have been this same little boy. It was for the reason of his death that his parents sold the house, hoping to get away from the surroundings which brought back so many sad memories.

As a child I had so many interesting things to do and so many interests and friends that only when something more mysterious or baffling would occur did I think of the spirit world as such. Being interested in gardening and art, I considered myself very much down-to-earth; even as far as reading was concerned. I much preferred "Betty on the Farm" to any kind of fantasy or fairy story.

Unusual experiences were always related to my family just as any other experience in life for which the child wants some kind of explanation and understanding. Fortunately they understood me well, understood the reality of the spirit world, and answered my questions wisely.

I remember quite well another experience, which also happened around the time my little spirit playmate had stopped visiting me. At that time I sensed a very strange presence which I did not seem to like, and there was no doubt about feeling something nearby that made me want to get up and leave what I was doing and flee from it. Wanting to run out of the room and out of the house, it was all I could do to stay still and try to find out why I had such an uncanny feeling around me.

The family cat appeared to feel the same presence. I watched my pet turn and look towards the stairway. I was startled to see the hair rise up all over its body and its back arch as if getting ready to spring at something unseen near that stairway. Suddenly, out of nowhere, an invisible hand appeared to reach out and smack the cat, sending it flying into the air with such force that it hit the side of the wall. It wasn't anytime before that cat got back onto its feet and dashed like a streak to the nearest door with me not far behind it!

Experiences like this and the one with my playmate, as well as other similar ones, convinced me at an early age that there were at least two kinds of souls, definitely good ones and some who were mischievous; also that some were actually seen while others were only felt or sensed.

Being brought up in the surroundings of a deeply felt and lived religion, it was difficult to understand why mischievous souls could and did annoy me. However, the more I thought about it, the more understandable it became. Since in life we do come in contact with so-called good and bad conditions around us, and as there are many times that we are annoyed by what is bad in the outer world, so it is also in the other dimensions.

Mama and Papa spoke so calmly to all of the members of our family whenever something happened in regard to the unknown. They both told of some of their experiences, and so, with their wisdom helping, we were taught to be as stoical as possible in all such situations. They also told us that there were many talents that the Creator bestowed on whomever he chose and that the spiritual sense or sixth sense was one such gift given to some in this world.

Papa had travelled quite far, and from time to time, he told us of his experiences. He had many unusual happenings with the sixth sense while working in the mines.

He often warned his fellow workers about the signs of danger underground, telling them to keep close watch on rodents and birds, who have an especially strong sixth sense for danger in mines. When the rats or mice began to scurry about, he could sense their fear of approaching trouble, and would warn the other miners before leaving himself. He always recognized another warning sign when he became aware of the scent of tobacco that his deceased papa used to smoke in his pipe. Whenever he caught a whiff of this scent, he gave notice of trouble approaching and sure enough, it would! A timber would break and fall, a tunnel roof cave in, or a dangerous gas would suddenly fill part of a mine. Thus, again and again his life and that of others he warned were saved just in time. Finally he decided, after one specially strong warning of this kind, that it was time to leave that type of work forever.

In my own experience and thinking, I have always called

many of my hunches an inner sense of warning. Many hunches come very far in advance and are often repeated long before the event occurs. Those hunches would be called long range hunches. Others come as a picture to the mind, which I call a "picture thought." Some dreams have symbols, which, when analyzed, are put together in my mind to form a meaningful pattern about a future event.

Many dreams are not prophetic, but others are very much so. In cases where I've had prophetic dreams, as a rule they have been dreams that have occurred in the early morning or just before awakening. There are dreams that recur over a period of time. After several months or even a few years, that recurring dream materializes in life. Warnings many times come twice, but sometimes a sharp warning is only shown once.

An example of such a warning is as follows: One morning, after everyone left the house, I was still in bed sleeping when I suddenly awakened and bounced up in the bed. I sat there staring at the form of a man dressed like a minister, who had just walked through the closed door, and yet was just as real in appearance to me as any person. Silently he stood just a few feet from the bed; then without saying a word, disappeared right before my eyes, as suddenly as he had appeared.

It did not take me long to realize why that spirit had appeared exactly at that moment. The room I was in was filling with the smell of gas, and I could hear the faint sound of gas escaping from the gas jet of the heater. I rushed to turn the gas off and open the window. The day before the gas had been turned off for repair work on the line. By mistake someone had turned the heater on, found it did not work, and forgotten to turn the burner off.

Spirits like these always leave a pleasant memory, even after you realize they are spirits. It is a comfort to know there is an ever-present and watchful, all-seeing eye, that sends a guardian spirit to watch and guide you while asleep or awake.

As time went on, the experiences became more startling,

but I'll still say one never receives more than one can endure. Just when I would think it was too much to take, it would ease up somewhat to give me time to relax and get adjusted to earthly surroundings until a new event would occur. The relaxation is quite amazing and well timed, since a guiding and unseen force seems to know when to take over in order to teach and guide you wisely. I would go along for weeks and months sometimes without seeing or sensing any phenonema, then, all of a sudden something strange would happen to make me aware of a spirit force.

I had an eager desire to learn what the world outside of my family knew and thought, so I'd inquire by asking questions of my friends at school and in my neighborhood. Their frightened attitude was very evident even at the thought of mentioning such a subject. However, some were a little braver than others and had questioned their parents to acquire some knowledge and understanding. The few that I had asked related how both parents had shut them up in their questioning and curiosity, which frightened them into silence. Thinking that the children were imagining such things, some parents quickly hauled their children off to a doctor, believing perhaps that their nerves were upset. Some were severely beaten and most told never to mention such a subject again!

Another child told of his family blaming his experiences on "imagination and an upset stomach!" Yet, with all the trips made to a doctor, he still had experiences with the psychic sense which no nerve medicine helped in any way. Realizing how it upset his family when he tried to explain these things to them he decided to drop the subject and to never mention any future occurrences. Hearing what happened to other children, I soon learned to keep silent and did not discuss my psychic experiences with outsiders for several years.

It made me wonder why the families of my friends took this attitude, but I was completely satisifed and happy with my own understanding family. I sensed that much real understanding in the home, was the beginning of a well-adjusted life.

This was long before I ever heard of the scientific studies of extrasensory perception, which is what we call the sixth sense.

I believe many parents and other members of families are destroying the gift of extrasensory perception as well as other talents a child starts to develop early in life. There must be many children with families that do not, or have no desire to, understand the gift of the sixth sense. They proceed to destroy or stifle it long before it has a chance to fully develop. These families do not recognize what the sixth sense means and no doubt have been taught to consider it fantasy, superstition, or a mental problem.

Almost every development starts in childhood, and the sixth sense starts very early, though many times it is not recognized until later in life. Then, again, there are exceptions to this rule when some people start to develop this power much later in life.

I began very early to recognize and sense the spirit gift. A brother and sister took notice of my hunches and other spiritual sensings, and watched very carefully for the outcome before even mentioning anything to me of their observations. Whether baffling or astounding, I learned and am still learning never to question the reasons of our Great Spirit. He knows his reasons and will in his own good time show me why. The desire to measure up to the job of life—the God-given work of each one of us—is ever present, and the need to become more and more purified in the spirit and in every thought is the desire of all that seek to walk the high road.

It is both interesting and amazing to find this same psychic sensing that I have reappear among my own children. My first little girl, Leota, often had many playmates, but, since many of the children in the neighborhood were of school age, she would be lonesome for companions to play with during the day. One day she suddenly announced that she wanted a baby sister or brother.

Later my sister and I were in for a little shock when hearing Leota say, "See baby! Baby flying up there!" as she pointed to the ceiling. "Baby has wings; see baby!"

Neither my sister nor I knew what to think about this, since my husband and I had been separated for over a year. Then, for several days, Leota would suddenly stop playing and say to us, "See baby! Baby turn on radio; I pank baby! Baby nice, too; I love baby!" She acted so real with the baby she saw in vision that it was quite amazing to us.

Then, in a few more days, no more than a week, I received a letter from Mama saying my husband wanted another chance at marriage. In two weeks we were back together again; this, after not hearing from him for many months. And in about a month and a half I was pregnant with the baby that Leota had seen in her vision. Thus, before my child was three years old, she had received the gift of spiritual sensing!

When moving into New York City, we stayed in an apartment my family had rented. Although they were moving into a home in the suburbs, they were keeping this apartment for a while, and my husband and I welcomed the chance to live there until we could get settled in a larger place. It wasn't long before our new baby girl, Lorena, started to speak of a former tenant, a friend of our family that had passed on a few years before either of our children were born. The friend's name was "Antelope." We were surprised to hear the baby, who could hardly speak, saying as she ran around the bedroom, "There man, there Antelope!"

In the days that followed, Lorena often talked to this soul, who appeared to be very friendly to her, and we felt it was a happy relationship about which we were not worried. How wonderful it would be if other parents lost their foolish fear of such things and allowed this sixth sense to develop in their children with understanding and love. I feel certain that much of the upset lives, fears, neuroses, and many unhappinesses of modern times are due to lack of understanding and of repression of just such gifts that are given to children and which, sadly, never have a chance to flower!

Chapter 3

Spirits Are Beings

> "Speak to Him thou for He hears, and Spirit
>   with Spirit can meet—
> Closer is He than breathing, and nearer than
>   hands and feet."
>
> from *The Higher Pantheism,*
> by Alfred Lord Tennyson

> "And ever near us, though unseen, the dear immortal spirits
>   tread;
> For all the boundless universe is Life—
>   there are no dead!"
>
> John Luckey McCreery

Ever since I had been able to toddle along, I had glimpsed a chief at times in vision and, although I stress the fact that there are many fine spirit friends that are not chiefs or famous in this life, I must say that this one chief, through the power of our Great Spirit, has often been by my side. I would see and hear White Feather, the chief, traveling along with me in my vision journeys.

In recent years a lady, while looking at me one day said, "An eye of a chief looks through you," and I soon answered her saying, "Through the guidance of our Great Spirit does the chief come near to me."

Some time later a medium told me she had many Indian friends and also many in the spirit world. While talking to me, she told me that a chief stood beside me who I had seen appear one afternoon in New York City in a restaurant. I hadn't told anyone of this vision, and this woman told me then that this chief was about 200 and that he had told me his age. I well remember him when he appeared near me that day, as I sat writing some poems that came through automatic writing. I believe they were sent to me through the spirit by him and others. Many of these spirits appear to me in vision with the scenery around them that is apparently of faraway or exotic lands, or of near lands, and some even of long ago while others are comparatively recent.

Then, as the medium thought for awhile, she said to me, "You hear snakes often at times, but should never fear them. You heard them by the seashore several times and, at first you were frightened." (This was true. I was frightened at first.)

When going to the seashore, and a couple of times since in the city, I have heard the snakes and accepted them, knowing if our Great Spirit, has his reason for me to hear them, as I pray, he will show me in time what I should know. Unlike the white people, who often think of the snake as something evil, most Indians believe the snake is a symbol or evidence of wisdom and healing. And at the same time that I heard the snakes, I also heard the birds. And I wondered about that, too.

Remembering how my little friends in school had been frightened about spirit talk, I hesitated to speak to people about my experiences. Gradually I began to ask more questions of others, and found, in most cases, the same reaction of fear. My knowledge of the spirit world was never pushed by myself, but acquired in a natural way. The family answered my questions only when something occurred that required their answers. This they did to the best of their ability, also giving explanations of somewhat similar experiences they had had. Not knowing for some time of books dealing with psychic experiences and phenomena, I had to develop my own way of understanding these things. A few movies or comedies that I saw, with ghosts running around in sheets, made no sense to me!

Going away in the summertime was always a pleasant adventure and something to look forward to. One summer we went to visit some friends in another state not too far from home. My sister and I had been visiting there for several weeks. One afternoon, while my sister had gone out to see friends, I remained at home to finish up some work. The family we were staying with also had plans for an outing and they left early in the evening. It was such a beautiful day that the people who occupied the top floor were out for a long drive. Each of them asked me to go along, but I had no desire to go out since I had so many things that had to be attended to; besides, I felt like spending that time at home.

Everything was going along fine for awhile, and it was some time before I sensed a quietness and was aware that I had recognized something like this before. I turned my thoughts to what I was doing and also turned on the radio for some company. I had been alone for quite some time before that stillness filled the air and I was trying to shake off the uncanny feeling that was coming over me. No matter how much I tried to relax, the feeling of an unseen presence became more and more evident.

Then, through all the quietude of the house and through that deep silence, an object that sounded like a can must have dropped from a table or something. This occurred on the floor above, because I could plainly hear this object roll back and forth several times overhead. The noise was startling and confusing. The object that I believe to be a can rolled back and forth more than just the normal number of times. But the rolling finally stopped and everything was quiet again. I went out into the hall to investigate and to call to see if anyone had returned home without my knowing it. Getting no answer, I was sure no one had come home, for it would have been impossible for anyone to pass by the door of our room without my hearing or seeing them, since our room was near the hall leading to the entrance of the upper floor.

Before I had a chance to get back into the room and settle down to what I'd been doing, I heard the soft notes of the piano being played in the living room downstairs. I was beginning to wonder if someone was actually playing a joke and perhaps hiding on me by now. At least, that is what I was hoping. Having that uncanny feeling about the place, made me suspect otherwise, though I still had hopes of being wrong in my thinking. Hearing the piano very clearly now, I wondered if it were possible for the cat to have jumped upon the piano and begun to walk across the keyboard, so striking some chords. I listened more intently, and recognized a tune. Then, of course, I knew for sure it could not have been the cat. I was positive that no one had come home yet, but I wanted to be sure no one was kidding or joking with me, so I called out from my door, and again received no answer.

Then I decided to do some detective work of my own, and began to explore the house. I went downstairs to make sure no one was there. I noticed the pet cat sleeping cozily in its favorite chair. The floor light was lit, as it generally was when someone was away. I could see plainly into the dining room, and entered it to make sure that I had every space covered. Then I went down to the hallway, which led back to the kitchen. I was suddenly hit with a cool breeze that came out of nowhere. Entering the hall on my return trip before going upstairs, the same cool breeze hit me again.

I can assure you the feeling that accompanies that type of breeze is very uncanny, and any other person with a keen sense will say, regardless of whether the presence is seen or unseen, that somehow it makes itself known. The breeze, in this instance, is not like the breeze of either summer or winter, nor does any imaginary or real fright of the physical world bring forth the same kind of atmosphere as does a passing disembodied soul. The feeling of goose pimples or the feeling you get when your hair rises a little may sound comical, but it is far from funny when it is happening to you.

I wanted to get away from that weird and breezy atmosphere. I did not wish to leave the house, so I simply hurried back to my room, feeling I would be more comfortable there. After I was inside I bolted the door! It seemed ages before my sister came home and you can imagine how happy I was to see her! When she first came in and knocked on the door, it was still bolted. She knew immediately something had happened, so I wasted no time in relating everything to her. As we discussed my experience, we both realized we had the same feeling about our quarters, something different than about any other section of the house. The strangeness about our room was felt from the very start. It was as though we were constantly being watched by an invisible being, and we confided in each other about our discomfort. This may have been one of the reasons we were so reluctant to unpack many of our personal belongings.

We had come prepared to spend the entire summer. Each day, as we would display a few more of our personal things, just to make the room a little more cheerful, we would feel so strange about doing this. There was no specific explanation as to why we hesitated this way about unpacking. So we just left things in our suitcases and took them out as we needed them. Outside of that, we were enjoying our visit, and looked forward to remaining all summer. We were not confined to our room, except for making changes and sleeping; therefore, we spent most of our time in different sections of the house or outside. If one of us desired a little quiet time or a nap, we spent it in our room.

But it was not too long before I was startled once again, and this time it occurred in my very own room. I had been out all morning and did not return until early afternoon after I had taken a dancing lesson. My feet were tired and I had turned one of my ankles a bit, so when I walked in I was bandaged and tired, and went straight to my room for a rest and a few hours nap.

I was suddenly awakened from a sound sleep by an uneasy feeling. At first, I thought it was someone else in the room speaking to me. Stunned and not fully awake, I bolted up from out of my slumber and looked toward the closet door. Standing there before me was a headless man, dressed in a blue suit and white shirt. He pointed at me and said, with a commanding tone, "Get out of this room!" I stared at him aghast, for what I saw and heard was so incredible. He repeated his command and pointed to the door. By this time I was as wide awake as could be. My eyes were still upon him as I was leaving the room as fast as my feet would carry me, bad ankle and all! I saw the outline of his head, then, as it appeared. But quickly, the figure disappeared before my eyes.

On my way down the stairs I encountered the landlady and began telling her what had happened. She encouraged me to describe the man in detail, and, in a short time, I was able to give her a verbal description of everything he wore, including the fact that he was a short man and that, by the tone of his voice, I recognized an accent. When I had glimpsed his head, I could see that his hair had been dark.

When I finished telling her about him, she burst into laughter, and I thought she would never stop! She was pleased to learn that I was psychic, and able to describe him to the letter. She startled me by telling me that my description of him fitted a former roomer perfectly. This man liked his room so much he considered this house his second home, even to the extent of paying for it when he was away on business for many months. The last time that he had gone out of town on business, she heard from some of his friends that he had committed suicide.

It took me a few hours to get over the ordeal in my room, the strange visitor, and the experience I had there. But like all the others I have had, it eventually disappeared and my mind was once again taken up with more pleasant thoughts. The evening was spent with everyone in the house joining in fun, discussions and plans for the following day. The earlier incident soon no longer entered my mind. Why and how we continued to keep that room after such an experience, I'll never know, as we could very easily have had another room in the house if we had wanted it. But we were determined to buck this condition and to convince ourselves nothing like this would happen again. At least we hoped it wouldn't!

In a few days another sister was planning to come out for a short visit, so we were busy making plans and waiting for her arrival. When she did arrive, we found much to talk about, as she had been away at school and we hadn't seen her for some time. There was no thought of mentioning anything about the strange events that had occurred. Everything was centered on our plans for the next few days. It turned out that we talked far into the night, laughing and giggling, when suddenly my sister stopped. "Gee!" she said, "this room must be haunted! I feel just as if someone is staring at me, and I'm beginning to get goose pimples and chills. Have any of you felt anything like this before in here?"

We tried our very best to calm her, then changed the subject. Neither one of us cared to mention the visitor we had had in this room, at least not that night. We had not informed the family about our experiences in this house, and hoped no one else did either, at least for now. We were certain that no one told our sister anything when she arrived, for she said nothing and evidently knew nothing until she sensed the strange presence in the room. We had rather expected something like this, however, for this sister was one that had shown the sixth sense from a very early age.

The next day, no explanation to our friends and landlords was necessary, as to the reason we were vacating their home— they knew! In fact, the landlady thought it was wonderful to be gifted with the sixth sense and wished she herself were so fortunate. We agreed it was nice, if one would not have to go through such unpleasant ordeals.

I would like to mention that when we came to this house in the early summer and the landlady gave us the spooky room, for the first few days I would see a cat dart out from under the bed, yet, when we were downstairs, we noticed that the landlady's cat was of a different color. I did not hesitate then to inquire if there were two cats in the house. She told me she had only one cat now. The grey cat, which I described, was a pet cat they had had a long time ago and it had passed away.

But, to get back to our departure, she realized that our minds were made up to leave, so she decided to tempt us to stay by offering us another room, hoping that at some future time we would return for a visit. She admitted, too, that she had heard that Indians were quite noted for having the sixth sense, and she was positive that if there was anything around a different room, one of us would eventually sense it. However, we decided to leave.

Events up to this point, including those of the past that had been a puzzle to me, were now beginning to shape up in my mind. I could see now that these souls as they appeared were of various kinds due to the lives they had led on this earth and the thoughts they had thought. Some of them became so obsessed with thoughts of certain things in this life that they were drawn back to the earth life even though they could not truly live it. They had never learned to seek for the higher world of the spirit that exists near our Great Maker, but had chosen the lesser and lower world because they did not understand. Perhaps some great unhappiness or desperate longing that could never be fulfilled drew them back, or some negative desire. Some such souls were definitely mild and harmless, such as a lady whose soft footsteps had once startled me as she stopped on the steps and landing outside my room at one house. Other souls, such as the headless man, who had so frightened me in the house where my sister and I went for the summer, were just as definitely mischievous or even harmful.

There's a big difference in how you feel when you meet a friendly and happy soul, and when you meet a troubled or misled soul. There are souls that can appear back on earth in the flesh after passing over and who are actually helpful and come to comfort you. You wouldn't realize they were not of this earth plane, unless you got that certain feeling within.

One time in New York it was such a beautiful day I decided to walk home. On the way what did I see but three fellows that looked almost like triplets. They smiled at me, and I smiled right back, and then I felt a sensation through my solar plexis, and knew for sure that these three fellows were appearing back on earth just for a short time.

As I walked along, I noticed that I had been transported several blocks ahead and that the three fellows were not far behind me. Then suddenly they vanished from sight. I felt as if I had known them before, since they seemed so friendly, and I felt happy to have seen them again.

It is evident to me now that there is one kind of good spirit that comes back from the happy regions to help the people of this world, especially all those whose hearts are open and who are trying to improve themselves. These are, in truth, messengers from the Great Mystery, and I feel they will help all those who strive sincerely and with all their hearts to do the will of our Great Maker.

There was one such wonderful being who sent me a message through the Holy Spirit. His name was Many Moons. A high spirit, working in faith through the kingdom, rarely tells you who he is at the very first. He lets you seek the holy light for some time before he makes his appearance or tells you his name. He wants you to first give glory and service to the Lord of the Silence before he shows you anything of himself. Thus, it was after I had prayed and worked for some time before Many Moons showed me that he came from the Holy Spirit, and this happened in the most beautiful and lovely way imaginable. I had a vision of a delightful sky, black velvet, speckled with star gems, showing several moons passing majestically through a series of filmy clouds, and then I heard the name spoken softly, "Many Moons." This vision was seen right here in my room in New York City where I am living as I write this. What a wonderful name that wise one has, he who has seen many years and taught the Indian people wisdom and still teaches me and others of this same wisdom! I felt his spirit reaching out to me with love and goodness way back in early childhood, helping to guide me with the holy light.

Spiritual Time Change.

Chapter 4

Beyond Space and Time

"And it shall come to pass afterward, that I will pour out my spirit on all flesh; and your sons and your daughters shall prophesy, your old men shall dream dreams, your young men shall see visions."

Joel, 2:28

The many spiritual sensings were well known to me from early childhood and then I felt the coming of another gift which was very awesome. I heard the announcement of trance mediumship. Hardly had I heard the voice say, "Trance, trance!" than I found myself in great wonderment, expecting something so awesome I had to walk around the room several times. Then I remembered the words Mama always spoke, "Be stoical, be stoical!" So, quietly, I went into Mama's room to chat awhile. As we talked, I began to remember sensing such a trance some months before, feeling far away from this world, and while I spoke to Mama, I began to feel as if I were suspended in mid-air, and far up in the universe.

Chatting again for awhile with Mama, I then felt the spirit tap me, and found myself on my knees at the side of the bed crying, "I am at God, our Great Spirit Creator's command, our Great Spirit's command!" When I got up to lie on the bed, Mama rubbed my shoulders, and in about an hour, I was ready to go on a trip I had to make into the city that day. As I got ready, I was startled to look at the clock, as I was keeping a check on my time for leaving the house, and there I saw a rosy hue cast around the clock, as I saw the hands swing around to the next hour.

"I must be mistaken," I thought, "perhaps the clock is wrong." But, as I was riding on the bus, I was sure I saw another clock change time. Then, as I got to the station, I stopped to look at a magazine, and also glanced up at the big clock on the building. Again the rosy hue formed around me and I saw the clock in the same rosy veil, while the hands of the clock swung around right before me.

As I arrived in town, I happened to notice the big clock on a building swing its hands and change time. When I came home, I told every one, "Time has changed. We are entering into a spiritual time change, and there is a rosy hue, as if I am looking at the world through rose-colored cellophane paper."

For the next two weeks I felt as if I were reading a story by picture and of some time far, far back, and I walked with the visions daily. I dropped many other things, such as reading different magazines, and did not even look at the headlines on the newspapers, while I turned the radio only to all classical music.

I was amazed at times to hear the heavy ticking of the clock, since I rarely noticed an ordinary clock ticking unless it was one so big the ticking would naturally be heard. For several days I only felt like eating a bowl of clear soup, and I would go for hours meditating in prayer. At such times one can sit at home and visit Rome, London, Egypt, Japan, and any place else on earth. Often, when I would be lying down just before going to sleep, I'd find myself traveling through the universe. In the next room, Mama would be singing a song as the spirit moved her. Often I told her, "Mama, you have been speaking through the spirit to all of us since we were babies!"

Then, one evening, a few days later, I was sitting at the piano, when, all through the room, cloud-like substances were floating in all directions. These clouds are heavier in appearance than those in the sky, and I had seen them as far back as I could remember, but I had never seen them forming around the room as they did at this time. I knew this was a spiritual phenomenon, but was somewhat frightened and prayed for forgiveness of all I had done wrong, that I could remember, and for all that I could not remember. When I spoke to Mama about this, she repeated, as always, "Be stoical! You know God never gives one any more than they can take and no more than they can stand."

I began having visions long before I entered grade school, but the big event that I am about to mention here, happened after I had my two children, and it went on and on for almost one month. As a great event comes about, it is always in tune with a mystical feeling which is accompanied by a complete change in atmosphere all around a given area, wherever you may be, in the house or outside. As this event casts it's shadow beforehand, it brings about the desire to enter into the silence and to become ever more watchful. The same mystical feeling came over me as this event started to unfold, and then the change of atmosphere followed through. I was startled when our house gave a big shake, then stopped. Looking out the window on that starry night, there appeared a book, not too far above the houses, flooded with brilliant lights. As I gazed at this large book, there on top of the opened pages, and in huge letters, the word "Revelation," in shimmering lights, was written! Now all that I could say was, "What on earth?" as I thought of this vision.

In the next three months I found myself in and out of trance often, and only through prayer was I given strength to understand. Fortunately Mama was always by my side, guiding me as she had done when I was a small child. I had seen many visions and spirit friends and had many strange dreams, but this was more awesome than anything I had ever witnessed before in my life. One afternoon I was astounded to hear voices coming from the nearby sea, saying, "We are Inca Indians that used to live here once." I said, "You did?" "Yes," they answered, "we used to live here long ago."

I had to hurry in to tell Mama, and as she was preparing lunch she said, "That is easy to understand." Mama took me over to a map on the porch, showing me the distance from New York to South America, where the Incas lived, saying, "Those ancient people had ways of traveling that we don't know about."

Later, as I sat at the upstairs window watching the beauty of nature, and the billowy clouds floating under the clear blue sky, I suddenly saw, as in ancient days, the many Indians performing their dances, and some beating tom-toms. And again I heard, "We're the Incas, we used to live here once." Every tree for miles, as far as I could see them, was swaying in rhythm, as if many spirits were in the trees, unseen, but swaying them. I was so thrilled that I went into the closet and brought out a little tom-tom to beat as I watched the wonderful ceremony that seemed to last for an hour.

After a little while I decided to go outside since it was such a beautiful day. I noticed there was not a neighbor in sight, and not one child out to play. When my brother came home from work, he was amazed that not one neighbor was outside on this beautiful day. It was then that I wondered if the neighbors had felt or seen these visions too.

Several days later I had a vision of a giant tree that would make the sequoia trees of California look dwarf in comparison. This beautiful and magnificent tree reached high above the clouds, and if it had been a starry night, I am sure I would have seen it reach the stars.

Many voices talked to me at different times, but I had to be very cautious when I answered, just as a baby learning to walk in life has to be cautious about missteps. I always called on our Great Spirit Creator to guide me. I took no chances even when I heard the voice of Montezuma, emperor of the Aztecs, speaking to me. I would reply only through the Holy One.

Mama being a school teacher, I told her I heard the voice of Montezuma, and soon I heard a voice saying, "Am I on a bed of roses?" Mama said that Montezuma said this as he was dying to the ones who were torturing him. But later I decided that this must be a different voice, though of the same time in history. This was because I learned it was Guatemoc Tzin, the last emperor of the Aztecs, who said this to another chief who was being tortured with him on a bed of coals and complained of the pain.

The Inca friends and Montezuma both said all the Indian tribes from North and South America will soon have a spiritual rebirth and be coming into their own.

During these weeks another awesome vision came through, as if the nearby bay had opened up so that I was witnessing the most beautiful baby swimming in the sea. Surrounding the holy infant, I recognized many of the largest sea animals I have ever seen outside of a museum, and even larger. The infant babe seemed to be about two years old in vision and he was swimming happily along. Startled, I called out, "Baby, baby!" Then, more startled, I heard him answer saying, "Don't worry, I have been doing this for millions of years!"

The babe pointed to a ship so large I could not see the end of it, and there I found myself with so many people I could not see the end of the huge crowd, and all races were together as happy as could be. What a beautiful vision it was of the brotherhood of man!

The "wonder baby," which was then being born in my soul, is awaiting birth and recognition in every individual being.

A few hours later, after being in and out of trance, and while sitting down listening to music, there on the wall of the room was a heart, alive and beating! I sat watching this heart pumping and breathing, for several minutes. There in the room, I could feel the magnetizing and electrifying spirit of the Holy One. Time seemed to stand still for a while after that. Since that time, whenever I feel the spirit moving in me, I find that I can get many things I have to do finished up quickly and easily.

I did not keep track of the exact dates, but as time went on I saw giants. Of course there is no such thing as the turning of something into nothing, so anything or anyone that has ever lived can be seen if one has the power. When our Great Spirit Father-Mother Creator gave me the gift to see these things through spiritual eyes, I found that seeing through this all-seeing eye, one can travel the universe.

At first, when I saw a giant, I was frightened, just like a child; then I remembered how my parents told me, "Have no fear. Conquer fear so that nothing can come between you and God, our Great Spirit Creator, and let our Great Spirit lead you all the way."

Fears are demons that put one into darkness and the many fears hold one in chains. Fear brings worry, nerves, the jitters, envy, lust, jealousy, illness, selfish pride, power-madness, prejudice, anger, lost hope, lack of faith, hurt pride, and many wars and other violence. How wonderful, I thought, if this world would start out to conquer fear by eliminating it and let the holy flame come into every heart and soul.

As I was taking trips often through the universe, fear had to flee from me on these flights that I soon learned were called "astral flights." On such flights one had no time for fears, as you see the beautiful sky spread over the earth as a canopy. Under this I again saw a magnificent and lovely tree reaching to the heavens, looking like the Tree of Wisdom. Sometimes I saw the miracle of the sun bouncing, quite a phenomena to see!

There are two stories I have to tell that illustrate the return of the Indian spirit and the great awakening that is coming. One night, to my surprise, I found myself in a dream so vivid that this is one dream I shall never forget. I looked about at a big fair. The scenery was more beautiful than fairyland. I remember how the sky was so lovely that I had to gaze at its rich and fathomless blue for a long time. Tents, gorgeously decorated with geometric designs, horses that pranced as if they were alive, antelopes that leaped over the endless prairies, buffalo bulls that charged feathered hunters, and many other animal figures on the tent sides, made that place of my dream thrill me with the feeling of reliving all the glories of the past of my people.

In the openings between the tents were many tables and racks displaying fine skins, tobacco bags, bows and arrows, lances, drums, beaded work and many other beautiful artifacts and art pieces of the many Indian tribes. Then I noticed the truly noble Indians who tended to the displays or walked about, all wearing most magnificent regalia of fringed and beaded buckskins and many feathers, their dark faces filled with light and joy, their voices ringing with spirit and their laughter like most glorious and happy music. This great Indian fair covered a space of ground as far as I could see, and there were thousands of Indians besides the ones that had their work on display.

I walked over to one of the nearest stands and gazed at the many articles of beadwork, telling the lovely woman standing there how fine this artwork was. I admired many articles, such as moccasins, jackets, skirts, baskets, and so on, when she startled me by saying, "You can do this kind of artwork too. Come back to us and our way of thinking and we will teach you. You will receive many inspirations through your dreams. I will send you many ideas."

When I awoke the next morning I started in right away to make many different types of beadwork, and until this day I have received many ideas for such work in dreams and visions. I believe this will be one way the Indians will teach us of this generation how to get back much of the ancient arts and knowledge that have been lost since the conquest. The pathway was opened completely for a continual contact with the wise ones. Many phenomena of this sort kept coming through, so I knew that many of the ancients of all races wanted to speak to me and through me, and that the Indians wanted me to be in tune with my ancestors so that I could speak for them to the world as a medium and through the power of faith in our Great Mystery Creator.

The ancient ones prophesied to us long ago that the dawn of a new day would soon be peeking over the hill of history, to shine brightly on men of all races, and that the Indian, who has at times wandered in the darkness of despair, will come to know that the Great Spirit Mystery has a plan for the coming of sunshine again.

The second vision of the return of the Indian spirit happened one day when Mama and I, and another friend, were visiting the American Museum of Natural History in New York, and enjoying the many relics there. As we came into the room where the Indian displays are shown, we stood before a glass case with two statues of Indian women working. One was a grown woman and the other a girl. On display with them were the types of baskets made by their tribe. As I stood there, suddenly the statue of the lady who was sitting, opened her eyes and without moving her head looked up from her basket work and smiled so sweetly and pleasantly at me she seemed like just any other living human being. Then she dropped her eyes and instantly appeared as a statue again! I stood unable to move or look away, and Mama said I was "transfixed."

In that fleeting moment I sensed quickly that this woman (I had stopped thinking of her as a statue) had a secret which she was revealing to me in that wonderful and pleasant smile. As I stook there motionless, startled and amazed, Mama turned to me and said, "Did you see that woman look up at you and smile?"

I stopped being transfixed and turned to cry, "Mama, did you see that too? Did you see her look at me?" She not only repeated that she saw it, but also proceeded to show me exactly what the woman in the case did.

Later we told the nearest guard what we had seen. The guard did not seem to be shocked or even skeptical in the least, telling us that several Indian guards who used to work in the museum had reported that they had heard and seen strange phenomena in that room, and had given up their jobs

Regeneration of past culture.

there, evidently in fear. He told us how many of the visitors liked to hear stories from the Indian guards about the different exhibits. It was too bad these Indian guards had to leave and be replaced by guards who were not bothered by the phenomena. I felt that this fear which made my own people leave their jobs was caused by lack of understanding of their own spiritual sensings and insights.

Mama and I often told many people of this experience, especially members of the many tribes we met, who were very interested. All agreed that this Indian statue coming to life and smiling was a wonderful omen, but many asked me why I did not think to speak up and ask her, as she smiled at me, what she wished to reveal. If I had spoken to her in the name of our Great Spirit, all said she would have answered. I had to admit that I was speechless at the time—transfixed. But, even though I did not think to ask her a question, the spiritual sensing united our thoughts and she knew as well as I knew, at that moment, that the time will not be long before the awakening of the Indian race.

Another symbolic meaning of seeing the statue come to life is that soon the Indians will no longer be like statues shown in museums to the curious, their glory apparently lost in the past, but would fully come awake to all their marvelous potentialities for good. When the Indian seeks sincerely for spiritual power, it will grow and grow, but *he must open both his heart and mind and seek as he has never sought before.*

When in tune with Great Spirit Gitchi Manitou, one is always on time; when out of timing, one may wait for years until getting back in tune with the Holy One. There was a time when, waking up in the morning, I had the feeling that I was traveling the "road of time" far, far back into the centuries. Then, as I was taken back through the years, while Mama sat near the window right here in the heart of this great city, I suddenly turned to her and another lady that was visiting us and said, "There are no trees on this busy city street, but do you hear the leaves of the many trees rustling in the breeze? I hear the sounds of many leaves, I see, as I walk around this apartment, a forest of trees and the Indians living as in olden times here and for miles around." "We see nothing," they said.

"Hear the trees; hear the leaves swaying in the wind," I said. Again Mama and our friend said "no." Then Mama said, "Everyone doesn't always hear what is heard by another being, but, when God wants you to see and hear, he can, and will, open up your eyes."

Soon Mama was again looking at the passing parade of people that daily go by this home, and she asked me a question about someone she saw across the street, and I answered her. But soon I was back on the "road of time." Again I asked her whether she felt the breeze that was becoming chilly and the strong winds I felt in the apartment, as I saw ice-covered lakes and rivers and seas from coast to coast. Again she and the other lady said "no." Then I heard the words, "Wisdom! Wisdom!" and then, "Regeneration! Regeneration!"

Soon after, a familiar vision came, and there went the neighborhood! In its place, a forest of trees appeared just as far as I could see. I turned to Mama and said, "Where are the buildings, where are the people, and do you see the tall forest outside?" She said, "No, but now I do hear the leaves and feel the wonderful breeze flowing in through the open window." After a moment the entire forest vanished, and everything was as usual—as if nothing had happened outside.

Now who but our Spirit Creator can erase a scene and then transport one back in time?

The scene soon turned to the forest view again, and that was when I saw the sky just full of Indians all dressed in full regalia, waving and smiling, and it looked like millions of them!

"The Indians are coming back!" I cried. "I am so glad! Did you hear this, the Indians are coming back! But, how is this really going to happen?" I kept asking. "Just how is this going to happen?" Then I stopped short, since I never before questioned our Great Spirit's wondrous works. So I said, "I had better not start now to question God." Mama answered, "That is right, and always remember, God in his own good time knows what to do; and it has been predicted that the once noble Indian will come back into his own."

One of my experiences several years back in trance was, when looking out the window one beautiful moonlit night, to see a cloud larger than any house around that area floating down the street. I kept watching the cloud for several minutes. The night was very clear, all except for this cloud of vapor that seemed heavier in substance than a real cloud. I felt a thrill of tremendous awe a few moments later when I saw an eye as large as a plate floating into the house.

At other times as this eye appeared, I would often glimpse the vision of a very large ship that seemed to have no end. On the ship many, many people were seen of all races and nations, as happy together as one big happy family. Everyone was going to that huge ship and I was hoping that many I knew would be there, and I met some of them. I believe this is the ship of a new world faith that will unite all religions and races as one.

The next scene was a beautiful and most wonderful vision. As we came out of much turmoil and storm, in the midst of what seemed just an ordinary neighborhood and as the mind's eye came into focus, a beautiful city appeared, moving down as if it were on a giant platform. Then it covered the entire area far and wide. As I gazed in amazement from the window for several minutes, I then decided to walk outside and view the glorious gardens and orchard, full of trees, vines and plants covered will all kinds of lovely fruits and flowers, such as I had never seen before. What magnificent beauty!

I can certainly understand that this erasing of a scene or condition is the working of a higher intelligence which reveals what this world should be through the eye of spirit.

That night I saw a vision of a dove flying near me, even though I was not near the window, and I took this to mean the Great Spirit was telling me of the coming of peace.

The Oneness of Mankind.

Often our Creator shows the same vision more than once, so when the next vision came, I recognized the beautiful and enormous ship that I had seen before with the many people of all races gathering upon it. Now this visional faculty is the eye that I had mentioned before, which sees into the reality of the greater world or kingdom of heaven. These visions are so greatly impressed upon the inner mind, that they can never be erased or forgotten.

Again one evening, as I felt the vibration of the spirit through my feet and legs, the moving spirit came up and enfolded me as I saw a big cloud around the room. On the table appeared suddenly a large telephone of a type I had never seen before. But just before it appeared, I had started to sing a song I heard once before that I call "The Royal Telephone."

That night as I was going to bed, I looked out the window and saw a most beautiful sight, the star-studded sky with castles floating in it. Then soon there again appeared the eye as large as a dinner plate. I finally told a lady that I had seen this large eye several times and she said, "Do you know that is the cosmic eye, the eye of the universe?"

Do you know that kindred spiritual souls meet on the lighted highway? That is why they sometimes feel natural with each other the first time they seem to meet. Friends in the spirit are meeting with each other from all parts of the world, more so than ever now, since the dawn of a new day is peeping over the hills.

Another time, and on a Sunday morning, while we were getting ready for breakfast, I sat down a moment to glance at the Sunday newspaper. This thick paper was full of many pictures and notices of exciting events that would eventually come true, I later realized. At the time I told my brother, "You should read today's newspaper, it is most scandalizing and many people in the government and other offices have black eyes, like they have been in fights." He hurried in to read the news, and I started to feed the children. Then he came back into the kitchen saying, "There is no news like what you said you read in this paper." I was stunned to see the paper had not one article or picture in it I had seen. We looked everywhere in the house for the paper I had seen, but never found it.

It was that morning that I noticed my brother move away from the kitchen window and then tell me, "Come down, come down; don't break the silver cord." I answered him, saying, "The silver cord? What do you mean?" He just hurried to make me some toast and gave me some coffee while he started to cook eggs, and said, "Eat!"

I said again, "What is the silver cord?" since I had seen something like a light, long thin line that was illuminated, and at times, several of them. He answered, "That is the cord of life." For a whole year he never mentioned anything about why he hurried away from the window to tell me to eat; then, one day, he said he saw me high up in the sky just as he was looking out the kitchen window that morning, and was worried.

I had often mentioned that I see pictures in the ether. Then a woman said, "You're reading the Akashic record." This record is a wonder to behold. These live scenes move in and through the home, the apartment, the neighborhood, and also throughout the world, and through the universes. Wherever the visioning eye goes, you go along with the scene. It is then that you meet events of the past, present and future, since the all-visioning eye knows no limitation of time or space.

It was often during the time of these visions, that the cloud-like substance would flow in and out of the windows and throughout the house, vanishing then appearing again and again. With these clouds, the eye like a golden ball of light as large as a dinner plate, came into focus, staying for days, hovering just a short distance above my head. There was one such night, when I just couldn't seem to get to sleep, so I stayed up to read awhile. It wasn't any time before something seemed to beckon me to the window, and looking outside, what did I see but this form of a cloud flowing down the street towards our home. "Now just what was this?" I thought, and turned off the light. Then I sat in a chair to think. Often I turn everything over to the Father within, and that's exactly what I was doing when I met our Father face to face.

I remember saying, "Are you my Father which art in heaven?" Then out of my mouth and through my whole body poured the words, "I am your Father which art in heaven." The words that poured through me were imprinted so deep, that I can never again call any man "father" on the face of the earth.

"Call no man your father upon the earth; for one is your Father, which is in heaven." *Matthew,* 23:9.

I will never forget the experience of meeting our Father face to face. I saw myself as both grown and at the same time as a child between the ages of two and three. I felt more like a little tot, and the joy I experienced was so joyous, it is still indescribable. I felt so comfortable and so relaxed and happy, it seemed as if I were sitting on the lap of the Father, looking up into the all-seeing eye. I have never been as happy! The feeling and the vision stayed for days!

In the next few days came a vision of many children running down the streets with trumpets blowing—thousands and thousands of them. The all-seeing eye seemed to expand all over the world with the children running down the streets with trumpets!

Just as long as you think of yourself as anything other than a child of God the Father, you are in trouble. *Only the child knows the Father.* Ponder this statement until the meaning is thoroughly revealed to you.

"Verily I say unto you, whosoever shall not receive the kingdom of God as a child, he shall not enter." *Mark,* 10:15.

Jesus gave us the "Lord's Prayer," which reveals the true relationship between Parent and child. It is often that we hear these truths and still do not grasp the full meaning until we receive understanding.

It was after many strange experiences, that I began to inquire of my friends in different tribes, if they too, knew of these psychic worlds. I was delighted to learn they did and that we were all in accord in our thoughts relating to the spirit world. We had all had some frights at times, and some things were very appalling, but the nature of spiritual awareness they all understood. Some of these friends were gathered from different sections of the country, as far as South America in some cases. Yet our thoughts were the same and the spirit world was spoken of with ease and with an awesome tone, and at times with great wonderment.

It is one thing to see or feel the happy events that are coming with joy, but it is most sorrowful to sense something sad coming to your family or friends. To see in vision and in dreams the future passing of a sister, or a parent is a sad experience. Only with prayer could I stand the waiting period, and then the time afterwards I had to ask for strength to dry my tears. So did I see in advance the passing over of my dear papa and mama.

The vision eye brings in one picture but not all at once. Then, as each picture is brought in through the spirit mind, the vision pattern begins to form, just as if one were putting together a picture puzzle. There can be no probing, since the Great Spirit mind knows just how much to give you until all the parts become focused back through the mind's eye into a meaningful whole. These sensings and impressions build a spiritual awakening gradually over the years. So, for example, I am coming to know thousands of friends in the spirit, so many I cannot count them, who work with you without showing their faces; then, all of a sudden, you see a vision and then see a face in the holy light.

On the following page is a poem I wrote called "Mystic Eye."

Mystic Eye

Great Spirit opens up your inner eye.
Through eye of soul you see.
That's only when you believe in Thee.
God says, "Believe in me."
The mystic eye through spirit is shown.
You can sit at home and visit Rome.
To Alaska, Egypt, London, Japan
Through spirit plan, see all these lands.
There is nothing that spirit cannot do
Spirit raises the dead and can awaken you.
Spirit can teach you to understand a foreign tongue
There's nothing new under the sun.
You're given dominion recognizing only one Father Creator
Then you are surely in Great Spirit's favor.
You must have heard you really are the *Word.*
And know you are not one of the "lost herd."
From the higher plane that you have found
You then will stand upon the higher ground.

Almost two thirds of spiritual sensing is in vision. One is two thirds awake and one third sleeping when this happens. At times, just as the body grows and develops in faith, so the sensings develop and you are unaware of this developing until the sensing grows upon you. There is a feeling, at such times, of a very thin veil that seems to cover the face and head to the shoulders, and feels like the very thinnest of hair-netting.

I had pondered this visional faculty that had been with me since early in life, and didn't know what to do with these visions. Somehow I sensed they were for a reason, since wisdom comes at any time in life.

Indeed, after many visions I decided to look for help. I wanted to understand more about trance, so I turned to parapsychology research for more knowledge. An appointment was made for me with a world renowned medium who interviewed me. Right away she said, "Do you know that the Inca Indians stand by your side?" And as she was looking startled, I answered, "What's wrong with that?" When she said, "That's the highest mediumship on earth," she startled me! She later told a friend of mine that I had the largest mystical eye in my forehead that she had ever seen.

The medical doctors who were interested in parapsychology invited me to spend one week in a hospital with three specialists to work with me. I had my own room with a private bath and a sitting room. The specialists took only a few tests, then I was handed a tablet and a pen. I was asked to write down some of my experiences, or whatever I desired to write. The head specialist finally told me that I was transported back in time, and also forward, and, "There's no telling how far back or forward you can go." I wondered how they could know this, since I had not mentioned this to anyone there.

Then another day, he told me, "Your people are the most ancient. They were before the Hebrews." "Whee!" I told him, "Now you must be a lost tribe of us!"

While I was in the hospital, the specialists would come in at any time, and one day they told me that I was appearing on two floors at once. They had come down to check me out, and were surprised to find me still in my room. This scene was really comical! To see one doctor rushing off to check the floors, and seeing me there, while the other specialist stayed to watch me as I sat in the room.

They were puzzled because this happened several times in the week while I was there. They didn't understand what it was, and at first I didn't know exactly what it was either. But I did feel it was something new coming into my experience and remembered a similar feeling the year before when I had seen someone dressed just like me, and who looked just like me, but was more beautiful, appearing right in front of our house where I lived on the beach.

I saw her just as I came out the front door and I walked up to her and asked, "Who are you?" She was standing near a beautiful chestnut brown horse, and she looked right at me and didn't answer. Then she and the horse both vanished. I thought at first that she was my twin sister who had passed over when she was an infant, but then I thought, "But why is she wearing the same clothes I am wearing?" I had a very vague thought at that time about my higher self, but didn't think about it again until months later when we had moved to New York City and there in the apartment I saw her again. She just walked through the door, wearing the same clothes I had on that day, and this time I asked her, "Are you me?" Then I said, "Or am I you?" Then she vanished again. A little while later I became aware that I had seen my higher self. The real me. The real inner self appearing outward. The self that knows itself.

Later I wrote a poem about this experience:

Real Self or Joyous Me

Somehow I knew I'd met *my self*
In spirit too, also the word made flesh
The higher self and spirit true
The greater self, that's the all-self too.
She did not have to say a word
    but the "inner voice" was what I heard.
I sensed she's that inner me of course
Through spirit mind heard the "still small voice"
She came another time then I knew
The time to rejoice was right here too
The spirit mind had sent her releasing
    false self on it's way
And I give thanks and gratitude
    with shouts of "Happy days!"

I put the memory of these appearances together with what the doctors had seen, and as I thought about it, I understood that they were seeing the spirit self that I had seen—my higher self. I didn't tell the doctors this at the time, but as I thought about it, I knew there was a reason why they had seen this vision.

I recognized the rebirth of the spirit coming into being to all mankind all over the world.

One of the reasons I had gone to parapsychology research was to find out how to get out of what felt at times like uncontrolled trance. Even though the doctors and the mediums had directed me through several steps; when I left the hospital I still felt that trance was uncontrolled at times. Shortly after my hospital visit, I found myself in a bookstore picking up a book called "The Inca World." I read that the Incas prayed to the *supreme light of the universe*. That ended my uncontrolled trance states forever! It was beautiful, as if the Incas had directed me to that book. As if they had handed it to me as a gift!

I can only say that my experience developed from my firm belief that our Creator can do anything, and with Great Spirit God, there's nothing impossible. This knowledge is brought forth directly through pure spirit, and is beyond the psychic senses, the astral plane, and beyond all scientific knowledge in this visible world. In the visible world, time is measured in terms of days, hours, months and years. Now in the infinite, there is no time, only periods called eons of light.

Modern science is very young, but spiritual psychic science is as ancient as the human race. The new science often doubts the value or reality of the science of the ancients without genuinely investigating it. It would surely be wiser and more scientific to seek carefully for understanding with an open mind and heart.

Chapter 5

Fears, Follies and Side-Paths

"And they worshipped the beast, saying, Who is like
unto the beast? Who is able to make war with him?"
Revelation, 13:4

It was puzzling indeed to see the many faces here and
there among the crowd in the city, all distorted and most gruesome. I was so startled that I had to stand aside and gaze in
amazement, wondering at first if these many people had just
come from a medical clinic somewhere near. Then, in a
moment, I realized it was a vision.

It was so amazing. For one minute, the people in the
crowd looked quite natural; then, the next moment, the
gruesome faces appeared among them again, looking just like
people that are afflicted with leprosy. It was a horrible sight to
see beautiful women and handsome men change their
appearance so terribly before my eyes.

Another time, in the month of June, I was taking a stroll in
the heart of the city and this vision appeared again and
disappeared just as quickly—then appeared again.

I tried not to glance too closely at the ones on whom I saw
this mark. I sensed it was the mark of the beast, which is also
the mark of lust.

Lust indeed is one of the great follies to which many men
and women are now addicted, to the great harm of all true
family life. The foolish ones seek their own pleasures,
forgetting that the Great Spirit asks us to control and master
our desires.

I understood this revealing was for me to help many through the holy kingdom to escape from the negativity they had embraced.

There is much done under the name of spiritualism or metaphysics or psychology that is done purely for private gain or to get control over other people. With so many here in this world that have stumbled or are still stumbling off the straight path and falling into the arms of those who are like wolf people (the werewolf type, not to be confused with the wolf that has always been known as a spiritual guide). The time has come to speak strongly and to speak the truth.

Several friends I know have gone through many years of incredible and horrible torment because of being misled by wolf people. Some of the so-called "metaphysical" organizations are not teaching the truth, but are really organized to do things with people that would shock the witches of Macbeth! Truly they are teaching under blankets of darkness. Some of the things are so ridiculous, it would be comical if it were not so serious a thing. Many are pure superstitions of the most foolish sort. Often, when I hear of these "metaphysical" organizations, I see, with the spiritual eye, dark corners filled with webs like spider's webs, and of course, this vision symbolizes human souls caught in the webs of darkness.

When the ego, which leads one to be trapped like this, is in discord with oneself, the world and God, it is diseased, for one is not at ease when the ego is dominant. Ego is the wall that holds one to one's own way of thinking and selfish desires in spite of new and true evidence. Thus ego is the carnal part of mankind, which can only be overcome by seeking earnestly to be in harmony with the intelligence of our Great Spirit Creator. During these times of transition from one age to another, when the minds and souls of many are in turmoil because of doubts, cynicism, selfishness, and misunderstandings, I often hear the carnal speech of the flesh mind. But the Great Spirit guards us by telling us to watch our speech and thoughts carefully every minute and let the words of our mouths and the meditations of our minds become purified. Oh, what a trap the tongue, the speech, and the thoughts are when not thoroughly watched!

Through the carnal force, when one is separated from the holy light, one sees negatively, speaks negatively, and works with the carnal mind to become a dual personality. This force, in time, works through the whole body, distorting it and the mind in inhuman ways.

As you pray for yourself or anyone else to awaken and find the true path to the kingdom of God, never look back with any negative belief, but keep your eyes ahead on the light that awaits you. Never make a statement with a negative thought behind it or with backbiting against anybody, but think kindly and with love, and faith will bring an awakening at any moment.

If one suffers from remorse, our Great Spirit Father-Mother knows all of our weaknesses, so tell spirit how weak you have been and hold back nothing, as you release all of your thoughts, words, and actions into the care of our Creator, and go forth free. Pray often for others afflicted with illnesses and for the world in general.

With heartbreak we all learn to walk in truth, finding that heartbreak brings strength through wisdom. There is no one on earth that doesn't have some kind of heartache, whether sickness, fear, remorse, grief, or something else, before they finally turn to the holy kingdom, realizing that the royal guards of heaven are waiting eagerly to help them. In several visions, I heard the name "Royal Guards of Heaven" and I came to realize that these could be the royal guards that many people think of as angels. Is this why they say guardian angel?

There is much need of prayer for others. There are many people hunting for truth, while the pied pipers of disunity, negativity, and of narrow and petty doctrine try to hold them back.

One day, while straightening up the house, suddenly I heard through the vision mind, "Hallowe'en is an evil celebration." I paused to think, "Why am I hearing this when it is nowhere near Hallowe'en? What does this mean? Then soon I heard the words, "Costumes no more for Hallowe'en."

I remembered I had a witch costume for my baby girl that I had dressed her in last Hallowe'en. I hurried to find the costume I had packed away, and out it went into the garbage can. I piled other things on top so that no other child would find it. I had to tell my children why I threw the costume away, and that was when my little Lorena said, "God doesn't want me to dress like a witch, and no other little girl either."

Thus I sensed that Hallowe'en, which is celebrated almost like a national holiday, should be abolished. With more thought, I hope people will realize that dressing in costumes that portray negative characters can mark and influence one's actions. Thus, an innocent-looking celebration of trick or treat may set negative patterns of conduct. The way many often become very destructive and lawless on Hallowe'en nights certainly bears this out.

Given gifts of charms and medals, I often wore them. I have never understood their purpose, but some were beautiful, and many people carry them and wear them, so I often wore a medal on a chain around my neck. But still, as I prayed, I was seeking the reasons for these medals and charms. Every medal I was given, I carefully put away in my little purse until I desired to wear a different one. But then, I began to find fewer and fewer in my purse; then the purse was lost with the rest of my medals. Finally, the chain with the medal I was wearing was often breaking, so I replaced it with another chain. Then I noticed an oh-so-gentle tug at the chain, as if an invisible hand were loosening it, and soon I found myself without chain or medal.

I sensed from this that there is no luck in wearing a medal or carrying one. Medals and charms are worthless, as all are man-made, and our Great Spirit's blessings do not need these man-made attempts at luck.

Many people have crucifixes of all sizes hanging in their

homes and elsewhere, and naturally I had one of the Christ on the cross. Then beautiful ones of ivory, plastic, wood and metal were given to me as gifts. I had several in different dresser drawers, and one on the wall, but they all started to come apart, and this was not too long after the incidents with the medals and the chain.

Seeing so many of the crucifixes coming apart, with the Christ coming off the cross, I pondered the reason. Then, taking the parts up in my hands, I glued them together with the strongest possible glue. But soon, the Christ was off the cross again. I sensed very strongly from this that the Christ, our Savior Great Spirit, is rising. We should carry or wear the cross no longer, but cast our burdens at the foot of the cross and see that a new day is soon coming when all men shall be gathered together as brothers.

Mankind is created in the holy image, and when our steps and houses are in order, we shall emerge into a larger world where the petty things of the past shall be no more. Truth stands forever in the holy Word, and when we seek the truth in spirit, we will exist in divine order.

After inner-meditating upon the Father within, and this with understanding of just what the Father really means and represents, I was feeling uplifted as I went outside to get some fresh air. I had only walked one block, when I met a friend that I hadn't seen for some time, and was he tipsy! He could hardly stand up straight, but nevertheless, we were glad to see each other.

He mentioned that he was on his way to the restaurant across the street, so we went there to continue our conversation. It was decided in the restaurant that we would take a walk and go to a party where he could introduce me to some of his friends. A few moments after arriving at the party, which was in full swing, my friend took me aside and told me that as soon as I had met him he had become sober, and so had each one of his friends. I had even forgotten that when I met him he had been tipsy, and the same with his friends. So the Father presence is indeed powerful as the power is poured upon those we meet.

Once you realize that the Father is the creative principle, and is the one and perfect life of all beings—of every man, woman and child on the face of the earth—then it becomes so. You must believe it, recognize it, accept it, and realize it. When you realize it, it becomes real. When you know it, you don't think about it. It is in your consciousness, and its effect is far reaching.

The Indian's Potential Destiny.

Chapter 6

Visions of the Rising Thunderbird

"Wa-kon-da dhe dhu—Wapa-dhin a-ton-he."
"Father, a needy one stands before Thee. I that sing am he."
Omaha Tribal Prayer

"Their hearts, contemptuous of death, shall dare
His roads between the thunder and the sun."
George Sterling

Oh, how the wind of change is blowing over the world, and through the holy light, I see the prophet saints marching as each one appears in the holy flame. With all the nonsense talk and the struggles of negativity, there is a ray of light that is shining brighter and brighter. I see also the vision picture of a large bush, a rose bush—the thorns first showing and just a few buds peeping out, and now more buds appearing; then, finally, more buds that start to burst into bloom. There are thousands of souls that have been working in the holy light for years and more each day are turning to the lighted highway. How can anyone who listens with an open heart not hear the song of many souls rejoicing? The kingdom of the holy light is every-where to be found—WITHIN.

You have heard of space people and vehicles being seen, but do not worry about them. Concentrate, instead, on seeking the light of the world today, forgetting other entities that distract you from this path. If you seek sincerely for the holy light, then the voices you hear are of the higher orders of the spirit world.

World-wide events were coming back into my sensing. There is no special time or place for this spiritual psychic sensing to occur, as sensing is at any time and place.

Again I had the vision dream, seeing hundreds of thousands of children turning the corners of a street, running east and west, then into a connecting street they rushed, blowing trumpets. And since everyone is really a child, the stream of children of every age group seemed to never end. Then I suddenly woke up, knowing that this was a prophetic dream of the time when children all over the world would awaken to the new spirit. I also realized that the trumpet is a symbol of the new age.

I saw horses galloping in the sky toward the sunset. When they had galloped by, row on row, into the glorious colors of the west and disappeared, a blooming garden was seen flaming with yellow, crimson, blue, and many other colors of flowers across the heavens. I still wonder about the full meaning of this vision.

A large vehicle, like a chariot, with a huge seat in the middle and wheels on each side, appeared in the sky outside my window. There, in the immense seat, was a giant being. This was in the early hours of the morning, almost at dawn, and I saw this beautiful chariot plainly as it came close. As I was drawn to the window, it faded into the sky. I had been asleep before this happened and had risen to get a drink of water when I saw this phenomena.

Horses In The Sky.

In a dream I saw a bird cage and on top of the cage a shiny new leaf. I immediately sensed the turning over of a new leaf, and also the turning over of a new leaf in world conditions.

Words came to me in vision saying that many religious denominations will make many remarkable changes that will startle the world.

Another thought revealed to me at this time was that a nation is no higher than its womanhood. Why should woman be lower than man, when man is born of woman and woman is born of man? How can any nation be truly successful when the men of that nation treat their women like slaves, and how can a nation be truly successful where the women treat the men as if they (the women) are superior? We find that slavery is never truly abolished wherever one side dominates the other. Men and women are born to be equal.

One afternoon I could see the time of shorter working hours for all types of workers. Then, in a flash, I saw many factories and buildings being built nearer the suburbs and closer to where people did not have to ride to work, as many were in walking distance of their work. The cities I saw less and less crowded as the people moved to smaller places and spread out, with the traffic of cars and busses gradually becoming more uniform.

Not long after the vision of the shorter working hours, I saw the children attending schools for about 4 to 5 hours daily, and spending more time in the out-of-doors learning things.

Soon I saw and heard through the vision mind that the many children in orphanages would be adopted. I saw a child crying in an orphanage in a large room filled with many children who were looking on sadly or trying to quiet her sobs. Then I heard through the mind again, "Children will not live in orphanages; they will have homes with wonderful families."

I have also felt that children are upset because they are not told how we can overcome war. Since they expect war, they can see no outlet for the future. They realize the horrors and sufferings of war, they listen to the warlords who seek their own gain and to the misunderstandings between nations. Children need to be taught constructive ways to bring all peoples into harmony, and taught the glory of peace, that they may grow up to work with all their might for world unity and love, so there will be no war.

What, I was asking, will awaken millions to all of these wonderful changes that are coming? Then I sensed the spiritual change of time and later saw several clocks change time right before my eyes; first the clock in the kitchen at home swung its hands around and there was a rosy hue in the room. And so, as I have already reported, I saw many clocks change time in that same rosy glow.

The changing times are pepping up now in these last years, and I hear the beat of the tom-toms and drums of the universe as they begin to pound out the march of humanity into a new golden age.

From the beginning of creation, Great Spirit has continued to reveal his Word and promises to every nation and every race on the face of the earth. The Far East—where much is written of prophecy and vision—is bringing our Creator's holy Word back to the West. In the past, many Caucasians scoffed at these teachings. A large part of all biblical records deal in such prophecy and visions, but only a small number of people realize the significance of this or how many of these prophecies and visions have come true. The black race too, has large numbers who are still too materialistic, but now many are growing more spiritual and are beginning to unite with those of all races who think likewise, for in the world of the spirit, there are no color lines.

The Indians I also see awakening. From South and Central America and North America, I hear voices, saying, "We are not figures of clay. We are Quechuas, Mayans, Aztecs." The primitives from these continents and the surrounding islands are speaking through the spirit world, and have been doing so for years, but now more than ever.

It is wonderful to hear the ancients speaking of the glories of the past, but even more marvelous to hear them foretelling the coming soon of an even more glorious new age to bring a welcome change to this sick world of ours. Many chiefs and other high and noble spirits speak to me through the spirit, making my heart glad as they foretell that every race will soon be having a spiritual awakening, and come in tune with our Great Spirit Mystery. The spirit voices are saying, "Who can stop the rising tide of humanity, just as who can stop the rising tides of the sea?"

One day, as I started to pick up my pen and tablet, I heard the name "Tamanend! Tamanend!" repeated. I wondered who this was as I prayed. Next I heard "Tamanay! Tamanay! and then finally Tammany! Tammany!" like the name given to Tammany Hall in New York City. And then I knew that the spirit speaking was the Lenape Delaware chief, Tamanend. As I am part Delaware, this was a great thrill, and also to hear that the Indian spirit is coming back.

I saw the awakening of the American Indians in vision also when my husband and I visited his people, the Sioux, near Chadron, Nebraska. While there I watched the many faces of my husband's tribe, as they sat around looking very sad, as things were not going well for them. Then a vision came, their faces became entirely different before my eyes, so that the many faces were all happy, smiling, and contented. Then looking again at the real faces, I knew this was a vision of the near future. I was reminded poignantly of the day in the

Museum of Natural History, years before, when we had seen the statue of the Indian woman come to life before our eyes and smile, thus foretelling the wonderful times that are coming, ending the time when the Indian is looked upon as a museum piece. In a flash, I had known from her sweet smile that she was telling me, "I have a secret! You know this too, now!"

When I told a Mojave friend, Standing Bear, that this sleeping giant, the Indians of the Americas, is awakening to a new day, was he stunned, then amazed, a little doubtful, but hopeful. So he told me, "If you would go to the tribes and let them know this, it would be wonderful!" I thought for awhile and said, "I will add another prayer to my list, asking to be shown how I can take this gift of foreknowledge to the Indian peoples, and help to arouse them, just as I have been aroused by these visions of the last years, so that they too will pray and work for the great awakening."

Chapter 7

Revealing the Messianic Age

"Where there is no vision, the people perish."

Proverbs, 29:18

Lately, I've had more and more visions and revelations about the coming times. Sometimes Great Spirit speaks twice, and sometimes three times, revealing the same vision. We are now in the dawn of the messianic age, and, as these revelations came to me, I pass them on to you. They are directly from spirit, and as I hold these visions, focusing and inner-meditating on them, I learn more and more about their meaning and my true identity.

May these truths help you to recognize your own visions, and as you turn them over to the plane of pure spirit, may you come to realize the truth, in divine order.

Now there are many and many who have never experienced visions, and they can hardly conceive of such things as ever being possible. The visional faculty is the capacity by which we see through appearances to infinite reality; and through this single eye of spirit was shown to me the book of Revelation, surrounded with shimmering lights.

There was a time in between these experiences, that a neighbor asked me to go on an errand for her. She was one of those so-called members of the "rocking chair brigade" or senior citizens. While I was sitting there waiting for her to decide what she wanted, she began to talk about her aches and pains; and then in a moment, right before my eyes, she changed from head to foot into a beautiful and very youthful lady of about eighteen! I gazed and gazed in amazement until she asked me, "What is the matter?" "I was only lost in thought," I said, but did not reveal to her what I had seen. For a few days, this same vision appeared on many of the people I passed on the street.

Gradually, I began to realize that I must *hold* every vision coming from the spiritual plane.

For some time, as I had visions, although I thought they were wonderful, I didn't know what to do with them. And finally it came to me, *"Be true to your vision, and hold it."* Holding the vision brings it into focus. As the vision is held in focus, we bring it into manifestation for all to see, and then for all to manifest.

How many people are conscious of the inner world of the Father that is within us, and of the true understanding of divine principle?

The vision that the book of Revelation opened up was shown for a definite reason, to reveal the falsity about death, and the truth about life. Contrary to the belief of millions and millions of people, our Great Spirit Creator never calls anyone in death. God is not the author of death. The principle of life cannot be the principle of death. It's impossible. The Father is the creative principle, the life force expressing in all creation. The Infinite Spirit is the "Rock of Ages," the song that we should sing in life, and not for the departed, as is often done.

I need not go into detail concerning the many false patterns followed by mankind for centuries, such as, "Nothing is certain but death and taxes." Another false pattern that mankind has followed for centuries is reincarnation. When the truth about life is clearly known and understood, we will begin to see that death and reincarnation are not part of the

Creator's plan. Then Great Spirit's promise will be fulfilled, "There shall be no more death." *Revelation,* 21:4.

"Lord, what fools we mortals be!" (William Shakespeare). Fools to imagine that we are mortal!

"And this mortal must put on immortality." *1 Corinthians,* 15:53.

In spirit and in truth, we know that our Creator in no way has the form of a human being, and the "still, small voice within" of our Creator in no way has the form of a human voice. Prophets, mystics, seers, sages, and many such illuminated souls speak in a human voice, but *it is our duty to discern all through pure spirit.*

In tune with the Infinite Spirit, and hearing Nikole, a small child in the family who had just started in the second grade, speak out saying, "You know we must live life, and everyone in this family must live life," I knew as she spoke so sincerely, that she was definitely speaking through wisdom.

Wisdom speaks often through children, and when another child in the family, John, frequently and spontaneously spoke the words, "I love you," to us and to some others that he would meet, I knew that was also wisdom speaking.

The Child

It has been an accepted belief throughout the centuries, that the wisest were the older, more experienced people. This is not always true. Whether female or male, married or single, now is the time to *give birth to your identity.* "For unto us a child is born." *Isaiah,* 9:6.

As long as you identify yourself as anything other than a divine child of God, you are asking for trouble.

Entering into the consciousness of truth, we realize that the child lying in the manger of the soul is the embodiment of infinite good or God, awaiting our *conscious recognition* of its presence.

To be a child means to accept and recognize the *way of the Lord* (law) in one's life as a child of the infinite. The child is in tune with the infinite, from which all love and wisdom flow.

Our choice is *to be* or *not* to be.

If more and more chose to become impregnated, and give birth to their true identity as the divine child, what a more harmonious world this would be!

The grown child that knows his or her identity, reveals the "wonder child" in every field of creative talent. The divine child knows the Father as the creative principle, the life force expressing in all creation. The "wonder child" shows, as the saying goes, "The only difference between the man and the boy is the price of their toys." The only difference between the woman and the girl is the same.

The "wonder child" reveals the tomfoolery to the saying, "Once a man, twice a child," and the saying, "They are in their second childhood." What appears to be "second childhood" is actually a partial remembering of the childhood that should never have been forgotten, the original divine childhood. When people forget they're a child they lose their identity. The child lying in the manger of the soul is often neglected, generally given the silent treatment, left to starve, often badly bruised and battered. The babe, left as an orphan, given out for adoption, can hardly stand on its two feet.

Many people are now becoming aware of the "child within," and are beginning to work with this divine image; loving and nourishing and feeding it with understanding, so that this image of the divine child will grow in wisdom, and thereby take over the governing of the individual.

Identity

In this so called space age, mankind is seeking an identity. First, came the character in the comic book of superman, which was long before the space age. Next were Spider Man and Wonder Woman.

Small children often ask, "Why am I here? and "Where did I come from?" Now when we begin to recognize the universe as a whole unit, we realize more thoroughly the meaning of the principle of oneness. The spirit in mankind is one and the same as Great Spirit, thus we bind our individual spirit to Great Spirit Manitou, and become one and the same.

Our true identity then is spirit, soul, and consciousness.

Before we were individual beings, we were universal beings, and sent forth from universal principle or Father principle. The Father is the principle that sends us out into the world to manifest principle. Again, before we were individual souls, we were universal souls. This must be firmly established in consciousness.

Mankind was grounded, through disobedience to the law of being, or rather not knowing the true meaning of this law. Man is the image and likeness of God, and has full dominion over all of his conditions, be they mental, physical, social, or financial; this is the everlasting universal law of being. Thus, made in the image and likeness of our Father-Mother Creator as spiritual beings, it is through the radiant spiritual body, that the true astronauts will travel through space. Then, through the power given of the Father, mankind will overcome gravity.

The Calling

We've all heard of these statements, that someone has a "calling," or, "this was their calling." This calling can be the gift of art, writing, acting, music, public speaking, cooking, designing; the gift of an architect, an athlete, or anything that is one's greatest talent.

Some very gifted ones have been called even before the age of eighteen months, and others as early as the ages of two and three. These children perform so brilliantly, that they have astounded their parents, since the parents could not conceive that such a gift could appear at such an early age. This proves that wisdom is present at any age.

that wisdom is present at any age.

The child is close to the infinite, and expresses the desire of the Father within, the true heart's desire, and also the genius within, since their imagination is God centered, and is a wonder for all to see.

There are many, such as Ludwig von Beethoven, Rudyard Kipling, Leonardo da Vinci, Luther Burbank, Walt Disney, and many, many others who received the calling and answered the call. In fact, everyone in the world has a special calling; and it is up to each and every one of us to come into tune with spirit to receive our own calling.

True ministry is a direct calling. The seer, mystic, and prophet hear their calling at a very early age. With this insight, there is a hesitation for moments, knowing the tremendous responsibility that comes with these gifts. As time goes on, you must be true to your calling. Any doubt or hesitation brings momentary affliction which passes as soon as you realize your responsibility.

My awareness of the real teacher, the inner self, started from my first glimpse of the light shining from within. Then, when looking out at the world through a child's view, I saw many things and conditions that did not seem to be true or in tune with the glimpse of this inner reality.

There are many ways in which the call is received, since it is sent forth from the highest plane of spirit. It can come forth in a dream, from reading a book, from meeting someone for the first time, or from a parent or other member of the family, or from a child's suggestion.

"The Royal Telephone" must always be open to receive the call through the inner ear connected to the inner spiritual self. We have a choice to receive the message or not to receive it, but no one is ever completely satisfied unless they answer the call: "Your heart's desire."

Be conscious of the divine presence within your innermost being, and receive your call.

A Child's Belief and a Child's Wisdom

Every child should be given the understanding of our Creator, so that very early in life, this knowledge can be imprinted upon the child's mind to become a guiding light throughout the years.

Even as a small child, I could never conceive of the idea of God as "the man upstairs" who governs this world and universe. The Creator, I thought, must really be spirit that can move everywhere and do all things. Who else can teach the birds to fly and even to sing?

When watching the birds fly away in the fall, and return again in the spring, I was sure that they were shown just what to do, and when to do it by Great Spirit. I was absolutely sure that a giant paint brush was used to paint the sky and the sunrise and sunset, as well as every season. The spirit undresses the trees and bushes in the fall, I thought, and then the spirit dresses them again in the spring, and knows just where to place each blossom and leaf, then fills the many blossoms with wonderful perfume. Then, to me, the emerald green lawns, the roadsides and meadowlands, dotted with beautiful dandelion and red clover blossoms, have always been a beautiful sight to see. Many think of these plants as only weeds, since they do not know the wonderful value of these spring tonics.

Now how could anyone call a calamity an "Act of God," or say, "that's life," when something goes wrong? Great Spirit is good, I thought, so how can any of these things comes from Spirit?

When I was first beginning to read, how well I remember that I suddenly said to Mama, "How did the first man learn to read? When he was little, he had no books, so didn't Great Spirit teach him all that he had to learn?" She thought about it, and had to laugh at this statement, but told me that I had to learn to read nevertheless.

So, unknown to me at that time, I had actually made contact with the inner master that teaches all things.

The Mighty Self

It is through the mind or consciousness, that we come into the awareness of soul, and through the soul, the awareness of the mighty self or spirit. Mind and body are not separated, they are one. And that one is the temple of the living spirit.

Our body, given us of God is eternally in heaven. Tuned into divine understanding, we realize that the "dust from which our body is formed," is in truth the same radiant spiritual substance from which the universes are formed.

As the soul awakens, it understands the meaning of the allself, the higher self, as the eternal parent of all mankind. Real peace, happiness and harmony can only be found through *unity* with the allself, which the innermost nature longs for. Our allness can never be taken from us, but we must recognize it and release it into our life for it to manifest.

Declaring your eternal unity with your allself, allows the Father within to enjoy the Father's life in us and as us.

When we dwell in the house of our own inner allself, we dwell in the Father's house.

God the Father-Mother is the only selfhood, and manifests as us, so we are God's own selfhood made manifest, and God's selfhood is the only "us" there is.

Indeed, this divine "I" is our only selfhood, which is God within us.

Now, no matter how secure your position, family life, or social life may seem to be, without the guidance of creative principle governing your allself, it can topple over at any moment. The Father is the creative principle.

Let your soul be clothed with the power of the mighty allself. Again, "Call no man your father upon the earth; for one is your Father which is in heaven."

Our Father

Now along with divine understanding of the "Lord's Prayer," and adding the gifts of supreme faith and unshakeable belief, these two very valuable keys open the door to the kingdom of heaven. I sincerely doubt if ever again anyone on the face of the earth, would call any man "father," if they understood the true meaning of what "our Father" stands for. To call one's own parents Papa or Dad, Mama or Mom, brings into divine order the human relationship between child and parent.

There was a time when someone gave me an affirmation: "May the spirit of Jesus the Christ within me assert itself, now and always." Then one day I heard a voice speaking through my mind, saying, "Don't pray to me, pray to our Father." I never take a chance with any voice; so even assuming that it really was Jesus, I still turned that voice over to the pure plane of spirit. I did this numerous times, as I thought of our Father within. The voice repeated the same words several times, so I let go of the affirmation and continued to turn to the Father.

It was several weeks later that I had that great and joyous experience of meeting our Father face to face. Then I knew why Jesus wanted me to have this experience: to reveal the true meaning of the Christ.

Like many others, I had been praying to the man, which is a form of idolatry. Even though I had mentioned the spirit in this affirmation, the Christ ideal had not yet come into focus for me because I had held the image of the man, Jesus, in my mind. I now understood that I needed to pray to the spirit and not to the man.

We must live in the *consciousness* of "I and my Father are one." This is the law of attraction on every plane. Like attracts like. Spirit attracts spirit. Christ and the Father and I are one, and are identical in spirit. The perfect I AM has always been, and is now, and ever shall be, one with the Father within, and can never be separated from the Father.

Not only are we one with the Father, we in truth are

identical, since the Father within is our higher allself.

In all of the universe, there is *only one* selfhood; the very same self in you is the same self in the moon, the stars, the sun, the earth and everything that dwelleth thereon; and this self knows itself in every atom of creation.

This is the meaning of, "Love thy neighbor as thyself." Your neighbor is your self, and your self is your neighbor. This is why I never meet a stranger. I meet the one mind in everyone.

I Never Meet a Stranger

Since there's only one true self, the divine self is in everyone. I never meet a stranger because the divine self which is the master mind in me recognizes the divine self, the master mind, in you. It's impossible for me to meet a stranger, because I meet the one life, the only life that lives.

Harmonizing with the one indwelling spirit as my true identity, I meet the one true spirit within whomever I come in contact. Therefore, I never meet a stranger. I realize it is time to rejoice, as I look immediately to the light which emanates from my own being, and from the being of every individual, as being one and the same light. I realize completely I never meet a stranger.

True Liberation—The Self Illumined Law

Awareness of the truth of being is true liberation. *True liberty,* freedom or liberation means respect and consideration of others. If the liberation of which you conceive, restricts others, this then is a false liberty.

True liberty does not give a license to dominate, destroy, restrict, or restrain the liberty of others. True freedom recognizes the dignity of all through an inner understanding of our own inner selfhood, which reveals the selfhood in all beings on the face of the earth.

Mentally acquaint yourself with the self illumined law. Self preservation is the first law of nature, and to lose sight of the inner self is sure bondage, the beginning of enslavement.

That we have made "doing our thing," a primary value in our society, results often in people being more selfish. We are still attending the "masquerade ball" until we realize that there is but one self, and that one self is the divine true self of every person, which includes those in whom it does not yet appear, and those who know it not.

"The truth shall set you free." We are created as living souls, and the soul must be allowed to expand, otherwise it shrinks. The term "lost soul" is merely a soul that has lost sight of it's divinity, or the *fall from within.*

As we take a page from history (his or her story), we find that out of twenty-one civilizations from the beginning of the world, sixteen civilizations that have decayed were first enslaved on the inside, which then caused the loss of self-illumination, self confidence, self sufficiency, self determination and self expression; and all this decay ended the reign.

The Akashic Record

Since this record comes directly from the heavenly kingdom, and through the eye of the awakened and illuminated soul, no one can tamper with this record. Every vision is revealed for the betterment of mankind. Even the errors in history books are made known, and then corrected. It may be astounding to many, that someone can walk in the record and talk to the ones that lived in ancient days, just as if one were talking to a neighbor or a friend living today.

I was again transported back in time to the glorious age of illumination. There, I met with people who had for their use every invention known today, and others that are to be rediscovered, such as the many means of travel that are as fast as the speed of light.

The Age of Illumination

We have heard often of the many ages, such as the stone age, the caveman age, the iron age, the age of the dinosaurs, the biblical age, and so forth. But how many have heard of the age of illumination, the time when everyone lived according to divine principle?

There is nothing *new* under the sun, and this being so, when we recognize and operate with the finished kingdom, and see our Creator's work as finished, we then come to understand that the kingdom of heaven is within our very own being, and thus we find heaven on earth.

Generations of Adams and Eves—The Adamic Age

There was a time when everyone sincerely loved divine principle, and definitely obeyed that principle of life.

Common sense simply shows that man did not live for just a short space in time and then "fall flat on their faces," as the story of Adam and Eve implies. There definitely was a time, right on this earth, when there were no wars, and happiness reigned supreme. And for thousands of years this was the way of life for all.

We often hear of archeologists that study the people, places and customs of the past. The past becomes alive and audible once again, as the archeologist is transported back in time. Does anyone question how they become aware of each and every detail of the past ages? It is then that the past becomes the living present, and we find that in God centered imagination there is no time or space.

Now anyone with divine understanding of the divine or

higher self which is in each and every one of us, and who becomes aware of its operation and expression, will not be surprised that this inner self can multiply and can transport one back in time, and forward in time. It can also appear in several places at the same time, and be active.

The time in the adamic age when people lived definitely with divine principle, reveals the first man born was the Christ. Now just how many mention that Eve (symbolized as the blue-bird of happiness), also was the first woman born as the Christ? Thus, there were generations and generations of Adams and Eves living in paradise, the Garden of Eden, as the Christ.

As they heard me speak often of Christ and Christianity, several Natives (Indians), finally asked me why I spoke of this religion, since Christianity, Christ's teaching, is the religion of the Caucasians. And then what about that joke, "Who is that white man, Jesus, all time broke?" I reminded them that many who call themselves Christians, and even many that teach this religion, do not know the true meaning of Christianity or what the word Christian stands for. When thoroughly understood, this religion is not just for one people or nation, but for all people and all nations.

The Christ

The true meaning of the Christ: The Christ is the central cell of life, the light out of the cosmos, the *divine central spark of life and love.*

As we act upon the acceptance and recognition of the infinite presence in accordance with *divine love,* the Christ is born into our life and experience. It is then, as we turn toward the *central spark of light and life* and recognize and accept it, that we no longer need to enter reincarnation.

Before we became individual beings, we were universal beings. Jesus Christ is the name of the law that is written within the center of the innermost being of every individual ever created.

The Christ child is sleeping in the souls of millions yet unaware that the name of the law is within.

It doesn't matter who they are, what they are, or where they are on the face of the earth; those who fail to recognize the beautiful drama of the higher self in every man, woman, and child, or in the stories of Jesus the Christ, Quetzalcoatl, and all the prophets and saints of every faith, as well as the seers and mystics of every nation, fail to recognize the absolute reality of their own true higher self.

The term, "only begotten Son," has confused many, but with understanding, the begotten Son represents the one relationship that every individual has with our Creator Father, Supreme Being, Great Spirit. Just as we speak of the Father and mean Father-Mother Creator, so when we speak of the Son, it also includes both male and female. Jesus Christ was, and is conscious of his relationship and oneness with the Father, and that is what gave him, then and now, his power; and that is also what gives each and every one of us our power as we move into our own Christ consciousness.

In ancient times when the prophet Dekanahwideh recognized this higher consciousness in himself, and brought the "Good Tidings of Peace and Power" to the tribes of the Iroquois, he said, "I will go and visit Tyo-den-he deh first." (Tiodenhe'de means, "He, who having died lives again," also, "He resurrects"). The missionaries who later wrote down the story thought that "Tyo-den-he deh" sounded like the same higher consciousness that they called the Christ, and used it as a name for Christ. (Reference: Parker, Arthur C. "Origin of the Confederation of the Five Nations," in *Parker on the Iroquois,* edited by William N. Fenton. Syracuse, N.Y., Syracuse University Press 1968, p. 68).

The teaching that all men are equally the children of the one Creator, is as true today as it has always been. The innermost nature of everyone is the same. There is nowhere in Christ's teaching that claims that he has any more power than any person can have; so if we abide by his teaching and accept his word, and put this teaching into practice, then we, too, become the Christ. We must definitely live the Christ life in thought, in word and in deed.

Awakening of the Soul

The soul is the spiritual part of a person, as distinct from the physical. "For what is a man profited, if he shall gain the whole world, and lose his own soul?" *Matthew, 16:26.*

A most important knowledge is the understanding of the soul. A soul has to be alive, illuminated and emancipated to function in divine order. If it doesn't function, it shrinks. Millions and millions do not know they have a soul, and the location of the soul is beyond the understanding of still more. Frustration, depression, discontentment and just about every problem of humanity is caused by lack of education of the soul.

Not in tune with the higher vibrations, misled souls are tangled up in delusions of *sense belief,* and like milkweed and dandelion tufts, can float around and attach to others that have never heard of their divinity.

We've heard of the saying, "wandering soul," and that is exactly what the soul does, and often. Often on its journey while one is asleep, or at times while one is awake, the soul can, and does, meet up with another soul that, too, has lost sight of its divinity.

Misled and Earthbound Souls

Common sense will tell you that *anyone,* at any time, can become "possessed" when leaving the soul open to be tampered with by an intruder. We've all heard of the earthbound souls that do not want to give up their attachment to the possessions they once had here on earth. We've also heard of "haunts," and haunted places. Books have been written about these places, and a special report was sent out from Washington about haunted houses all over the country.

Since the time when man lost sight of his innermost nature, there have been countless stories of people being possessed by these misled souls. There are hospitals, jails, prisons, and institutions filled with people that have been bound by these alien invaders, since they do not know what to do to help themselves. We've also heard of people with personality changes, and of ones with split personalities, and others with bizarre behavior. With some, there is dope, drinking, and then suicide. These are all actions expressed by earthbound souls. There's only one way that souls become earthbound, and that is by holding on to possessions. They want to hold on to a person, a place or a thing, even a belief system. Like attracts like, and these alien invaders are drawn to people on the earth plane who do not understand divine law.

The Identity of the Soul

To be in tune with divine law, we must *consciously* remember that we come from the unknown, and before we became individual souls, we were universal souls. In understanding this, we take our place in the universe. Here on earth, we must live as microcosm constantly and consciously in tune with the macrocosm.

Many teach that "all is good," and that "God is everywhere." Well, so is the "light of truth." But these statements are not enough. Unless you *consciously* connect with the God within, there is no illumination. It's like the electricity in your home which is available, but if you fail to make a connection and do not turn it on for the light to shine, you can still be in the dark.

Yes, the teaching must include "all is good," and "God is everywhere," but *only* when and where this great truth is *realized, recognized, and accepted in our consciousness,* does it work in the affairs of our lives.

Remember, "It is the Spirit that giveth life." In all substance there is a single soul, the universal soul, and our true identity is spirit, soul, and consciousness.

As our soul belongs to our Great Spirit Creator, we must return it to its original source even while we are living on this earth, so that we may experience a life of freedom, peace, and happiness. It is in this freedom of the Father within, that *we* are free.

Freedom comes from giving up the sense of the importance and the attachment to personal possessions, and knowing that all we possess of position, talent, home, wealth, family, and all activity, belongs to the universal mind substance which we call God.

It should be known that the soul never dies, and that there is freedom of the soul as it seeks peace, emancipation, and illumination from the spirit within. Each individual soul must be clothed with a consciousness of its mighty self. Only through spiritual sense are we able to discern the true identity of the Christ in other souls. By inner-meditating on the inherent light, and just letting it come in, we come into tune with divine law.

Inner-meditate on the soul clothed with the mighty power of the allself.

The Door

I was working a puzzle and occasionally watching a television program, when suddenly at the top of my forehead, a door opened just like any door of our home or apartment; and there appeared a solid blue color, like the pale blue light of dawn, as the door opened and closed several times. I was astounded!

"I am the door," is a statement which I have heard. Now

who would believe that there are such things as doors manifesting from our inner self?

As visions appear, and also during experiences with the Akashic record, words, phrases and sentences seem to fall out of the ether and are related to these visions or experiences. "I am the door." *John,* 10:7-9; "Ye everlasting doors." *Psalms,* 24:7

Many great truths are heard just as soon as we enter this world or earth plane, and it becomes natural to repeat these truths from time to time with little understanding, if any. Therefore we must reach an inner knowledge and understanding to become the truth in action and then to manifest truth.

I AM is the door in every soul that must come forth in consciousness through expression as wisdom, love, and truth.

As we seek to illuminate and emancipate our soul, we become a free soul, and the very door of our soul opens up; and the all knowing, all seeing, all hearing, all wise, and intelligent spirit enters in. "I am the door," expresses the one who is the great opener of these heavenly doors. The eye of the soul knows no limitations of time or space. We open the door of our soul—the everlasting door—and walk out into the light of our divinity.

The Eye of the Soul

Now, if every book upon the face of the earth should vanish, and this includes, all the holy records which Great Spirit has given to mankind since the beginning of creation, and even if one has never read or heard of the Word; the illuminated, completely free spiritual soul can, through the eye of the soul—the deeper mind—see and read the book of life. And we can know the Word, and the promises that are recorded and written within our innermost being.

The eye in the forehead is also called the cosmic eye, and

it becomes focused on the plane of the eternally perfect, seeing directly into the kingdom of heaven.

Even as a child, and not knowing anything about the soul, the light glimpsed occasionally shining in front or at the side of the forehead was a delight to see. And even then, I sought to be in tune with that light. Indeed, this light shining through the soul is wisdom; and that light is also the presence of knowledge within the individual consciousness. Light or knowledge is God, since God is knowledge.

There comes a day, even though your soul has not totally awakened, when you meet your higher true self, the most beautiful self. And it is impossible not to know that this very self is seeking its rightful place as you.

When leaning on the Infinite Spirit, we're leaning on the Rock of Ages, the All in All, and the All as All force that occupies all images and all space; and which reveals the pattern to us. Just like making any garment with a pattern, the Holy Spirit places the pattern before us and shows us how to put it together. As we start to recognize our higher self and the infinite power within, we begin to be about our Father's business.

A true spiritual being is not disturbed by any activity of the spirit, knowing fully that all things are possible in the manifestation of spirit; so when the spiritual joy body is duplicated, this does not come as a great surprise. And yet it is always a wonderful surprise when your full consciousness realizes what has happened!

You can be busy with your daily tasks, while the eye of the soul lets you know where the spiritual joy body is. There can be more than one body duplicated at the same time, doing Great Spirit's work wherever it appears. What a pleasure to watch the spirit in action!

When someone tells you that they were visiting a certain state, and saw you there, and you know you hadn't visited that place, you begin to know that they have seen your spiritual joy body, and that you, as this duplicate self, were there. How can one explain this so-called miracle to someone that wouldn't believe it in the first place?

After several people tell you of their experience of seeing you in various places where they have been, you know that it is time to be about the Father's business of living, giving and receiving, since the Father is the principle that sends us out into the world to manifest principle.

These appearances in different places were revealing a pattern showing the "coming events that cast their shadow beforehand." There must be a thorough study of the activity of the spirit through inner-meditation and contemplation, since there is more and more knowledge to learn on the path. "Faith without works is dead."

This self may have several names, but it is always the same self, the higher self, the Father-Mother within, that does the work.

You must realize, recognize, and accept this self.

Jesus sent his higher true self to heal and help many. Quetzalcoatl spoke the Word the same as Jesus did, and his word should have been written and sent out into the world. Jesus never wrote the Word that he spoke either, but others, hearing his word, wrote what they heard.

No man or woman is the Christ. *The activity of truth in the consciousness of each individual is the Christ in them.*

New Age

The coming of a new age does not happen overnight, or even suddenly, since it is the breaking down of an old worn out system making room for a new order. Mankind does not readily accept changes of habit and belief; and, as we have seen from history, the Mayans, Egyptians, Romans, Chinese, Toltecans, Greeks, Africans, Peruvians, and many others, were no exception. In the present day, there are also many who do not believe that there is to be a change.

As this new age dawns, in spiritual sensing and in vision, I am reaching back for the truth, and bringing it in. I'm seeing the light that lights all mankind, and expressing it. In the beginning, Great Spirit God gave his truth to man, and the truth was in every language, whether it was written or spoken. I don't know the words for I AM or "the perfect word" or "the Christ" in the many Indian languages, because the meanings of these words have been lost, although they certainly exist, and can be found again as we seek them through truth. Meanwhile, one language is as good as another to me, since the meaning is the same in every language.

The word "religion" is derived from the Latin word "religare," meaning, "to bind back to the truth." As religion is tampered with, it no longer holds truth.

Mankind may think that church can be separated from state, or from a system of government, not knowing that the true church is not just a building entered to worship, but the church of your own true self, binding back to the law of being—man is the image and likeness of God, and has full dominion over all his conditions.

The word "spiritual" is derived form the Latin "spiritus," which means spirited, alive, energetic, full of vigor, animated, and lacking nothing in life; which is our true destiny.

Spirit is Principle or First Cause, our Parent.

Now, how many living in the jungles, mountains, deserts, or other places thoughout the world have heard of the Greek word, Logos, which means "the creative Word?" This also applies to the misunderstanding of the word, Christ, which means "the perfect Word—the light."

To tell someone, they are the Word and the law, they would think you were talking tomfoolery, and they would either move away from you or perhaps flee!

Not knowing of the supreme Christ law of divine freedom and harmony, it is not surprising to know that those who suffer from the delusion of hidden insecurity, fail to recognize this law as the law of liberation.

All of these laws are related to the one universal law of life. As we turn back the pages of history, and if we are wise, alert to everything that takes place around us, and do not sleep in the dawn of this new age, we will learn from the mistakes of earlier civilizations.

All of the great civilizations that once flourished, fell due to two main reasons: the overemphasis of *sex, and it's misuse,* and *acts of mental malpractice*—the twisting of truth for personal gain.

Sex

Sex is with us from the time of birth, since it is related to the universal life force. There are three phases of sex: spiritual, physical, and mental-emotional, which must harmonize with the universal life force.

However, each phase of sex is spiritual.

Physical sex is based upon the body energy and desire for self-expression, and with some, the desire to reproduce. The mental-emotional sex drive is the passion and feeling expressed as ideas, talents, and ability to produce these ideas in a successful creative way. The spiritual sex drive is the passion that seeks God the Father, and hungers to find the truth of all creation in every detail.

Each phase is given us of the Creator and governed by universal law and supreme intelligence. The spiritual phase of sex (Christ consciousness), leads us to the awakening of soul consciousness, through which we act to saturate and absorb our physical, our mental-emotional, our astral and our etheric bodies into our glorious light body (spiritual joy body), which has no limitations of any kind.

In divine understanding, we recognize the universal laws of rhythm and gender which govern the physical phase of the sex drive. The universal law of polarity governs the mental-emotional and personality phases of passion and sex drive.

Polarity is known to be a basic factor in human behavior. When we enter into the *paradise state of mind* (heavenly state), and use our inner faculties of love and wisdom, expressed in a harmonious way, both physical and mental-emotional phases of sex become balanced. Balanced means stable, harmonious, and orderly.

Actually the divine principle is the law of harmony, balance, and order. Every condition in life must be definitely governed by the law of balance. We see today many people, including some of fame and fortune, who have not understood this law, and have gone haywire.

The Kingdom of Heaven Within

The paradise state of mind has never left this earth. It is remembered through the kingdom of heaven within us, though many have fled from paradise, thinking it must be somewhere in the skies. Others are awaiting the return of paradise here on earth.

Heaven is the everywhere present, divine harmony, and order within the individual being right where you are at this very moment.

Of course, it is not easy for some to believe that heaven or paradise is nearer to them than their own breath or closer than hands or feet.

Through my conscious awareness and spiritual vision, I saw the royal guards of paradise. I recognised that they represent the eternal rules of order and right which heaven itself has ordained right here on earth. The royal guards of paradise allow only the individual being as a pure soul to enter the kingdom. "In the Father's house there are many mansions."

It is well to understand that this path to the kingdom is very straight and narrow on the way.

As we dwell in the spiritual soul, we become living souls, and it is then that the soul hungers and thirsts after righteousness. Just as the physical body hungers and thirsts for nourishment, the soul hungers and thirsts for the Word, which becomes a daily habit, even though at first you are unaware that the Word (promises and law) is pouring from the soul into the glorious light body. Then both soul and light body become a prayer constantly in action.

The Word

As we embody the Word in our consciousness, we become the living Word. We can hear the Word, read the Word, and sing the Word, but only the actual practice of the Word brings results; this is the Word in action.

The Word is the true food of the soul, wherein abide the Great Spirit Gitchi Manitou (the Father) and the divine central spark of light and life (the child).

The words of St. Augustine, "Too late have I loved Thee, for behold, Thou wert within and it was without that I did seek Thee." We then realize, "Though Christ a thousand times in Bethlehem be born, if Christ is not born in thee, thy soul is still forlorn."

The glorious awakened spiritual body finds the Word so tasty, it gorges upon the Word, due to the undernourishment of long neglect.

There is the daily bread which consists of physical food, shelter, clothing, money, and all of the other attributes which contribute to our well being. Spiritual bread must be added to complete this menu. The daily bread also means the food for thought such as harmony, perfect order, peace, plenty, joy, happiness, and freedom. Through the inner mood, the spiritual bread is a feeling of faith, understanding, truth, and real self-confidence in your higher self.

Let's Tell It Like It Is

The Word is wisdom that knows itself within us and as us. Mentally call upon inner divine wisdom, the greatest teacher. Together, the physical body and spiritual or light body *must* harmonize. In tune, the physical body, a garment covering our frame, and the pure garment of joy, the light body, *work* together.

Our daily feast then, consists of *hearing* the Word, inner-meditating on Great Spirit's exceedingly great promises, the *Proverbs*, and every word of God's truth. Reference, *Matthew,* 4:4 "It is written, man shall not live by bread alone, but by every word that proceedeth out of the mouth of God" (or Infinite Good, Great Spirit, or Allah; one and the same).

We must mentally feast upon the Word, mentally live and abide in the Word. Indeed, to become the Word is complete and total fulfillment. "Being born again . . . by the word of God." *I Peter,* 1:23. "Nourished in words of faith." *I Timothy,* 4:6.

Forgiveness and Thanksgiving

Many have asked for the reason and meaning of asking forgiveness when taking the life of an animal for food. The asking of forgiveness is the same as saying grace for that which has been provided for nourishment.

All mankind has a soul. *Everything* on the face of the earth has a soul. The subsconscious soul is included in every form of creation, there being only one life force, the only life that lives.

As we take of food for the physical body, the act of asking forgiveness for taking the life of an animal or plant is a recognition of the great principle that all life is one. Thus, thanksgiving is *every* day the inner action of a thankful heart.

Mother Nature—Mother Earth

The saying, "from dust to dust" or the term "dust of the ground" seems to confuse many. The "dust of the earth," simply means that every individual was and is *formed* of the universal radiant substance of which everything upon the earth and in the universe is formed. It is for us to acquire the right conception of this substance. Radiant substance is pure light. This radiant substance changes into whatever form given it, through a thought, idea or action. In the original state, radiant substance is formless and penetrates, permeates and fills the inner-spaces of all the universes.

Our appreciation and love for Mother Nature goes far back to the wisdom of the ages, revealing knowledge of this same radiant substance, plentifully supplying everything necessary for abundant life.

To love and appreciate Mother Nature is to know that radiant, divine substance underlies and supports everything in our world, and is none other than our Great Spirit Creator in action.

By turning to inner understanding of divine substance, our increased awareness reveals radiant substance as our willing servant, working with us and around us to provide everything necessary in life.

When you inner-meditate upon pure substance, you bring it into form.

The Body

We suffer only in the flesh, because "out of body," in spirit form, there can be no suffering. The spiritual self is detached from the physical or flesh form, but nevertheless determines and controls the health and every condition in every sense and detail, since this spiritual body is perfect.

This free, illuminated, spiritual self, or bright soul, is radiant light, taking on the color of the golden sun.

Radiant pure spiritual body substance is the same substance out of which all the universes are formed, and it flows through the creative principle moving through our body and being this very instant.

Our body must become totally spiritual, since there is no material in the kingdom of heaven. Now, the "body," not only means the physical organism, but also refers to mind, spirit, home, family, job, business, and the entire life and all the affairs of mankind.

The term, "earth," also refers to the same things.

We then realize that we are the embodiment of the omnific Word made flesh; thus, the Word is spirit and life.

This radiant light body is immortal, spiritual, indestructible, and cannot be harmed.

This is the same "body" that will conquer space and overcome gravity, as it moves through the power of the Father principle.

True Sun Worshipper

In ancient days, our Creator was called, "The Sun." The later biblical reference, "For unto you that fear my name, shall the *Sun of righteousness* arise with healing in his wings." *Malachi,* 4:2.

Sunday is the Lord's day, and the Sun is the sun of understanding. Let's set the record straight: the acceptance of our Creator as the Supreme Light of the Sun, and the only one relationship, the divine Sunship, was common knowledge. Divine Sonship and divine Sunship both have the same meaning as the divine child of God.

The Absolute Reality of Existence

Now upon every plane, there exists the spirit omnipresence, omnipotence, omniscience. We are constantly told to seek the kingdom of heaven within us, right here and now.

Since the Word has already been established in reality, earth is the starting point where we must enter into heaven within, without delay.

No one enters into heaven when leaving this world, unless they have already done so while here on earth.

As we turn within, and recognize our inner self, we can meet our Creator, but there is much work to do before we enter the kingdom, since each one of us is in reality an offspring of spirit and must become totally spiritual in every sense.

"In my flesh shall I see God." Job, 19:26.

In truth, we are pure spiritual beings, subject only to spiritual law, the law of love. Material becomes separated from spirit when we fail to hold in our consciousness the truth that all is one in God.

We have not been taught that there is but one body identified and individualized as each individual body, given us of God, and eternally in heaven. For centuries, having thought of a material body, we now must go through the process of removing this heavy shell by inner-meditating upon our glorious light body, consciously recognizing and accepting this body as our very own.

We endure in the flesh until the complete change takes over, but we do not suffer in vain—divine principle bears with us as we suffer on the way.

False teachers invariably try to persuade us either that we can be relieved of suffering altogether, can avoid it, or can gradually rise above it without fulfilling the law. This is why we often hear that, "Just as soon as someone passes out of visible world, they go directly to heaven." Again, *no one enters into heaven when leaving this world, unless they have already done so while here on earth.*

Real teachers show us that this suffering is essential for all of us.

"Suffer little children to come unto me, and forbid them not: for of such is the kingdom of God." *Luke,* 18:16. The biblical record can only be read and understood through infinite wisdom.

Now there comes the false teaching again, saying, "Those poor souls whoever they may be, have left this world and now they are resting in peace at last, they have nothing to worry about any more." Nonsense! Peace begins right here on earth!

Again, I need not go into detail concerning the many false patterns that mankind has followed for centuries. As mentioned before, when the truth about life is clearly known and understood, we will begin to see the falsity about death and reincarnation, and then the promise of our Creator will be fulfilled, "There shall be no more death."

Life Principle—The Promise of Great Spirit

The life principle that came to the planet millions and millions of years ago brought no death to the planet. The ungodly with their works and idle words called forth the death wish. Then the people started following these ungodly patterns which were not designed by divine principle. Divine principle is the kingdom of heaven on earth.

From the beginning, Great Spirit gave the *same truth* to all men and all nations: "For I have no pleasure in the death of him that dieth, saith the Lord God, wherefore turn yourselves, and live ye." *Ezekiel,* 18:32

"So, too, men die but live again in the real world of *Wakan-Tanka,* where there is nothing but the spirits of all things; and this true life *we may know here on earth* if we purify our bodies and minds, thus coming closer to *Wakan-Tanka* who is all-purity." —*Black Elk*

"There will be a spiritual conflict with material matters. Material matters will be destroyed by spiritual beings who will remain to create one world and one nation under one power, that of the Creator." —*Book of the Hopi*

"There is no death. Only a change of worlds." —*Chief Seattle.*

"And God shall wipe away all tears from their eyes, and there shall be no more death, neither sorrow, nor crying, neither shall there be any more pain, for the former things are passed away." *Revelation,* 21:4.

Scientific knowledge of living is recognizing the principle of life that stands under, and supports everything. Principle means: A truth and foundation of all truth; a rule of science, explaining how things act; a basic fact; origin—First Cause.

There is only one truth—the reality of person, place or thing.

Now, do we have the right conception of the Father? Do we realize "To know God aright is life eternal?" Do we really understand the law of divine principle? Through understanding and right thinking according to principle, we definitely know Great Spirit's promise to mankind *never* fails; and to believe is to know from the center of our innermost being that the life principle cannot break its own law, which is everlasting; and this law can never go against itself, which is the promise.

New Coming of the Christ Light

The spirit of the Christ has come to me in vision several times, the earliest at the age of nine. Many think that our Great Spirit Mystery could only come first at one time and in one part of the world and that his return would be up in the sky with great glory, but this is false due to the constant and natural longing of men to see the reflection of God in a sight of great material glory, not understanding that his spiritual glory is the only one that counts. Thus, many of the Bible stories of the Christ spirit's return are symbolic only and not to be taken literally.

When I first saw the light of Christ, it was so brilliant that I was for a short time blinded. The vision of the most beautiful lights, large and small, also appear near many that are awakening to the truth, and I call this "the highway of lights."

God's will is the only thing that should count with us, for when we are away from the spirit, in even the smallest way, we are like lost children. We must be obedient to divine law and glorify our Creator in everything we do. In seeking the kingdom and the holy Word, we become our Parent's true children and can help others by speaking the Word. All we can do then is pray that they will see the light, for they will have to enter into the garden of God alone, opening their hearts for the spirit to enter into their souls. And in this time, they need to stop listening to all words that divide mankind into petty parts, for Great Spirit is not small in this way, but seeks to bring us together in love.

The Christ appearing as the avatar, can and will manifest in different parts of the world at the same time. This is already beginning to happen. We are in the dawn of the messianic age.

DATE DUE

HIGHSMITH   # 45220